The Selected Works of Lin Biao
First Prism Key Press Edition 2011

Prism Key Press
New York, NY 10001
PrismKeyPress.com

ISBN-13: 978-1466481619

The Selected Works of Lin Biao

CONTENTS

Long Live the Victory of People's War!

Introduction

Fully twenty years have elapsed since our victory in the great War of Resistance Against Japan.

After a long period of heroic struggle, the Chinese people, under the leadership of the Communist Party of China and Comrade Mao Tse-tung, won final victory two decades ago in their war against the Japanese imperialists who had attempted to subjugate China and swallow up the whole of Asia.

The Chinese people's War of Resistance was an important part of the world war against German, Japanese and Italian fascism. The Chinese people received support from the people and the anti-fascist forces all over the world. And in their turn, the Chinese people made an important contribution to victory in the Anti-Fascist War as a whole.

Of the innumerable anti-imperialist wars waged by the Chinese people in the past hundred years, the War of Resistance Against Japan was the first to end in complete victory. It occupies an extremely important place in the annals of war, in the annals of both the revolutionary wars of the Chinese people and the wars of the oppressed nations of the world against imperialist aggression.

It was a war in which a weak semi-colonial and semi-feudal country triumphed over a strong imperialist country. For a long period after the invasion of China's northeaster provinces by the Japanese imperialists, the Kuomintang followed a policy of non-resistance. In the early stage of the War of Resistance, the Japanese imperialists exploited their military superiority to drive deep into China and occupy half her territory. In the face of the massive attacks of the aggressors and the anti-Japanese upsurge of the people throughout the country, the Kuoumintang was compelled to take part in the War of Resistance, but soon afterwards it adopted the policy of passive resistance to Japan and active opposition to the Communist Party. The heavy responsibility of combating Japanese imperialism thus fell on shoulders of the Eighth Route Army, the New Fourth Army and the people of the Liberated Areas, all led by the Communist Party. At the outbreak of the war, the Eighth Route and the New Fourth Armies had only a few tens of thousands of men and suffered from extreme inferiority in both arms and equipment, and for a long time they were under the crossfire of the Japanese imperialists on the one hand and the Kuomintang troops on the other. But they grew stronger and stronger in the course of the war and became the main force in defeating Japanese imperialism.

How was it possible for a weak country finally to defeat a strong country? How was it possible for a seemingly weak army to become the main force in the war?

The basic reasons were that the War of Resistance Against Japan was a genuine people's war led by the Communist Party of China and Comrade Mao Tse-tung, a war in which the correct Marxist-Leninist political military lines were put into effect, and that the Eighth Route and the New Fourth Armies were genuine people's armies which applied the whole range of strategy and tactics of people's war as formulated by Comrade Mao Tse-tung.

Comrade Mao Tse-tung's theory of and policies for people's war have creatively enriched and developed Marxism-Leninism. The Chinese people's victory in the anti-Japanese war was a victory for people's war, for Marxism-Leninism and the thought of Mao Tse-tung.

Prior to the war against Japan, the Communist Party of China had gone through the first Revolutionary Civil War of 1924-27 and the Second Revolutionary Civil War of 1927-36 and summed up the experience and lessons of the successes and failures in those wars, and the leading role of Mao Tse-tung's thought had become established within the Party. This was the fundamental guarantee of the Party's ability to lead the Chinese people to victory in the War of Resistance.

The Chinese people's victory in the War of Resistance paved the way for their seizure of state power throughout the country. When the Kuomintang reactionaries, backed by the U.S. imperialists, launched a nation-wide civil war in 1946, the Communist Party of China and Comrade Mao Tse-tung further developed the theory of people's war, led the Chinese people in waging a people's war on a still larger scale, and in the space of a little over three years the great victory of the People's Liberation War was won, the rule of imperialism, feudalism and bureaucrat-capitalism in our country ended and the People's Republic of China founded.

The victory of the Chinese people's revolutionary war breached the imperialist front in the East, wrought a great change in the world balance of forces, and accelerated the revolutionary movement among the people of all countries. From then on, the national liberation movement in Asia, Africa, and Latin America entered a new historical period.

Today, the U.S. imperialists are repeating on a world-wide scale the past actions of the Japanese imperialists in China and other parts of Asia. It has become an urgent necessity for the people in many countries to master and use people's war as a weapon against U.S. imperialism and its lackeys. In every conceivable way U.S. imperialism and its lackeys are trying to extinguish the revolutionary flames of people's war. The Khrushchov revisionists, fearing people's war like the plague, are heaping abuse on it. The two are colluding to prevent and sabotage people's war. In these circumstances, it is of vital practical importance to review the historical experience of the great victory of the people's war in China and to recapitulate Comrade Mao Tse-tung's theory of people's war.

The Principal Contradiction in the Period of the

War of Resistance Against Japan and the Line of the Communist Party of China

The Communist Party of China and Comrade Mao Tse-tung were able to lead the Chinese people to victory in the War of Resistance Against Japan primarily because they formulated and applied a Marxist-Leninist line.

Basing himself on the fundamental tenets of Marxism-Leninism and applying the method of class analysis, Comrade Mao Tse-tung analyzed, first, the mutual transformation of China's principal and non-principal traditions following the invasion of China by Japanese imperialism, second, the consequent charges in class relations within China and in international relations, and, third, the balance of forces as between China and Japan. This analysis provided the scientific basis upon which the political and military lines of the War of Resistance were formulated.

There had long been two basic contradictions in China --the contradiction between imperialism and the Chinese nation, and the contradiction between feudalism and the masses of the people. For ten years before the outbreak of the War of Resistance, the Kuomintang reactionary clique, which represented the interests of imperialism, the big landlords and the big bourgeoisie, had waged civil war against the Communist Party of China and the Communist-led Workers' and Peasants' Red Army, which represented the interests of the Chinese people. In 1931, Japanese imperialism invaded and occupied northeastern China. Subsequently, especially after 1935, it stepped up and expanded its aggression against China, penetrating deeper and deeper into our territory. As a result of its invasion Japanese imperialism sharpened its contradiction with the Chinese nation to an extreme degree and brought about changes in class relations within China. To end the civil war and to unite against Japanese aggression became the pressing nationwide demand of the people. Changes of varying degrees also occurred in the political attitude of the national bourgeoisie and the various factions within the Kuomintang. And the Sian Incident of 1936 [1] was the best case in point.

How was one to assess the changes in China's political situation, and what conclusion was to be drawn? This question had a direct bearing on the very survival of the Chinese nation.

For a period prior to the outbreak of the War of Resistance, the "Left" opportunists represented by Wang Ming within the Chinese Communist Party were blind to the important changes in China's political situation caused by Japanese aggression since 1931 and denied the sharpening of the Sino-Japanese national contradiction and the demands of various social strata for a war of resistance; instead, they stressed that all the counterrevolutionary factions and intermediate forces in China and all the imperialist countries were a monolithic bloc. They persisted in their line of "closed-doorism" and continued to advocate: "Down with the whole lot."

Comrade Mao Tse-tung resolutely fought the "Left" opportunist errors and penetratingly analyzed the new situation in the Chinese revolution.

He pointed out that the Japanese imperialist attempt to reduce China to a Japanese colony heightened the contradiction between China and Japan and made it the principal contradiction; that China's internal class contradictions -- such as those between the masses of the people and feudalism, between the peasantry and the landlord class, between the proletariat and the bourgeoisie, and between the peasantry and urban petty bourgeoisie on the one hand and the bourgeoisie on the other -- still remained, but that they had all been relegated to a secondary or subordinate position as a result of the war of aggression unleashed by Japan; and that throughout China opposition to Japanese imperialism had become the common demand of the people of all classes and strata, except for a handful of pro-Japanese traitors among the big landlords and the

11

big bourgeoisie.

As the contradiction between China and Japan ascended and became the principal one, the contradiction between China and imperialist countries such as Britain and the United States descended to a secondary or subordinate position. The rift between Japan and the other imperialist countries had widened as a result of Japanese imperialism's attempt to turn China into its own exclusive colony. This rendered it possible for China to make use of these contradictions to isolate and oppose Japanese imperialism.

In the face of Japanese imperialist aggression, was the Party to continue with the civil war and the Agrarian Revolution? Or was it to hold aloft the banner of national liberation, unite with all the forces that could be united to form a broad national united front and concentrate on fighting the Japanese aggressors? This was the problem sharply confronting our Party.

The Communist Party of China and Comrade Mao Tse-tung formulated the line of the Anti-Japanese National United Front on the basis of their analysis of the new situation. Holding aloft the banner of national liberation, our Party issued the call for national unity and united resistance to Japanese imperialism, a call which won fervent support from the people of the whole country. Thanks to the common efforts of our Party and of China's patriotic armies and people, the Kuomintang ruling clique was eventually compelled to stop the civil war and a new situation with Kuomintang-Communist co-operation for joint resistance to Japan was brought about.

In the summer of 1937 Japanese imperialism unleashed its all-out war of aggression against China. The nation-wide War of Resistance thus broke out.

Could the War of Resistance be victorious? And how was victorious to be won? These were the questions to which all the Chinese people demanded immediate answers.

The defeatists came forward with the assertion that China was no match for Japan and that the nation was bound to be subjugated. The blind optimists came forward with the assertion that China could win very quickly, without much effort.

Basing himself on a concrete analysis of the Chinese nation and of Japanese imperialism -- the two aspects of the principal contradiction --Comrade Mao Tse-tung pointed out that while the "theory of national subjugation" was wrong, the "theory of quick victory" was untenable, and he concluded that the War of Resistance would be a protracted one in which China would finally be victorious. In his celebrated work On Protracted War, Comrade Mao Tse-tung pointed out the contrasting features of China and Japan, the two sides in the war. Japan was a powerful imperialist country. But Japanese imperialism was in its era of decline and doom. The war it had unleashed was a war of aggression, a war that was retrogressive and barbarous; it was deficient in manpower and material resources and could not stand a protracted war; it was engaged in an unjust cause and therefore had meager support internationally. China, on the other hand, was a weak semi-colonial and semi-feudal country. But she was in her era of progress. She was fighting a war against aggression, a war that was progressive and just; she had sufficient manpower and material resources to sustain a protracted war; internationally, China enjoyed extensive sympathy and support. These comprised all the basic factors in the Sino-Japanese war.

He went on to show how these factors would influence the course of the war. Japan's advantage was temporary and would gradually diminish as a result of our efforts. Her disadvantages were fundamental; they could not be overcome and would gradually grow in the course of the war. China's disadvantage was temporary and could be gradually overcome. China's advantages were fundamental and would play an increasingly positive role in the course of the war. Japan's advantage and China's disadvantage determined the impossibility of quick victory for China. China's advantages and Japan's disadvantages determined the inevitability of Japan's defeat and China's ultimate victory.

On the basis of this analysis Comrade Mao Tse-tung formulated the strategy for a protracted war. China's War of Resistance would be protracted, and prolonged efforts would be needed gradually to weaken the enemy's forces and expand our own, so that the enemy would change from being strong to going weak and we would change from being weak to being strong and accumulate sufficient strength finally to defeat him. Comrade Mao Tse-tung pointed out that with the change in the balance of forces between the enemy and ourselves the War of Resistance would pass through three stages, namely, the strategic defensive, the strategic stalemate and the strategic offensive. The protracted war was also a process of mobilizing, organizing and arming the people. It was only by mobilizing the entire people to fight a people's war that the War of Resistance could be persevered in and the Japanese aggressors defeated.

In order to turn the anti-Japanese war into a genuine people's war, our party firmly relied on the broadest masses of the people, united with all the anti-Japanese forces that could be united, and consolidated and expanded the Anti-Japanese National United Front. The basic line of our party was: boldly to arouse the masses of the people and expand the people's forces so that, under the leadership of the Party, they could defeat the aggressors and build a new China.

The War of Resistance Against Japan constituted a historical stage in China's new-democratic revolution. The line of our party during the War of Resistance aimed not only at winning victory in the war, but also at laying the foundations for the nation-wide victory of the new-democratic revolution. Only the new democratic revolution makes it possible to carry out a socialist revolution. With respect to the relations between the democratic and the socialist revolutions, Comrade Mao Tse-tung said:

14

In the writing of an article the second half can be written only after the first half is finished. Resolute leadership of the democratic revolution is the prerequisite for the victory of socialism. [2]

The concrete analysis of concrete conditions and the concrete resolution of concrete contradictions is the living soul of Marxism-Leninism. Comrade Mao Tse-tung has invariably been able to single out the principal contradiction from among a complexity of contradictions, analyze the two aspects of this principal contradiction concretely and, "pressing on irresistibly from this commanding height", successfully solve the problem of understanding and handling of the various contradictions.

It was precisely on the basis of such scientific analysis that Comrade Mao Tse-tung correctly formulated the political and military lines for the people's war during the War of Resistance Against Japan, developed his thought on the establishment of rural base areas and the use of the countryside to encircle the cities and finally capture them, and formulated a whole range of principles and policies, strategies and tactics in the political, military, economic and cultural fields for the carrying out of the people's war. It was this that ensured victory in the War of Resistance and created the conditions for the nation-wide victory of the new-democratic revolution.

1. Under the influence of the Chinese Workers' and Peasants' Red Army and the people's anti-Japanese movement, the Kuomintang Northeastern Army Under Chang Hsueh-liang and the Kuomintang 17th Route Army under Yang Hu-Cheng agreed to the anti-Japanese national united front proposed by the Communist Party of China and demanded that Chiang Kai-Shek should stop the civil war and unite with the Communist Party to resist Japan. Chiang Kai-Shek refused. On December 12, 1936, Chang Hsueh-liang and Yang Hu-cheng arrested him in Sian. Proceeding from the interest of the entire nation, the Chinese Communist Party offered mediation and Chiang Kai-Shek was compelled to accept the terms of unity with the Communist Party and resistance to Japan.

2. Mao Tse-tung, "Win the Masses in Their Millions for the Anti-Japanese A National United Front", Selected Works, Eng. ed., Press, Peking, 1965, Vol. I, p. 290.

Correctly Apply the Line and Policy of the United Front

In order to win a people's war, it is imperative to build the broadest possible united front and formulate a series of policies which will ensure the fullest mobilization of the basic masses as well as the unity of all the forces that can be united.

The Anti-Japanese National United Front embraced all the anti-Japanese classes and strata. These classes and strata shared a common interest in fighting Japan, an interest which formed the basis of their unity. But they differed in the degree of their firmness in resisting Japan, and there were class contradictions and conflicts of interest among them. Hence the inevitable class struggle within the united front.

In formulating the Party's line of the Anti-Japanese National United Front, Comrade Mao Tse-tung made the following class analysis of Chinese society.

The workers, the peasants, and the urban petty bourgeoisie firmly demanded that the War of Resistance should be carried through to the end; they were the main force in the fight against Japanese aggression and constituted the basic masses who demanded unity and progress.

The bourgeoisie was divided into the national and the comprador bourgeoisie. The national bourgeoisie formed the majority of the bourgeoisie; it was rather flabby, often vacillated and had contradictions with the workers, but it also had a certain degree of readiness to oppose imperialism and was one of our allies in the War of Resistance. The comprador bourgeoisie was the bureaucratic-capitalist class, which was very small in number but occupied the ruling position in China.

Its members attached themselves to different imperialist powers, some of them being pro-Japanese and others pro-British and pro-American. The pro-Japanese section of the comprador bourgeoisie were the capitulators, the overt and covert traitors. The pro-British and pro-American section of this class favoured resistance to Japan to a certain extent, but they were not firm in their resistance and very much wished to compromise with Japan, and by their nature they were opposed to the Communist Party and the people.

The landlords fell into different categories; there were the big, the middle and the small landlords. Some of the big landlords became traitors, while others favoured resistance but vacillated a great deal. Many of the middle and small landlords had the desire to resist, but there were contradictions between them and the peasants.

In the face of these complicated class relationships, our Party's policy regarding work within the united front was one of both alliance and struggle. That is to say, its policy was to unite with all the anti-Japanese classes and strata, try to win over even those who could be only vacillating and temporary allies, and adopt appropriate policies to adjust the relations among these classes and strata so that they all served the general cause of resisting Japan. At the same time, we had to maintain our Party's principle of independence and initiative, make the bold arousing of the masses and expansion of the people's forces the centre of gravity in our work, and wage the necessary struggles against all activities harmful to resistance, unity and progress.

Our Party's Anti-Japanese National United Front policy was different both from Chen Tu-hsiu's Right opportunist policy of all alliance and no struggle, and from Wang Ming's "Left" opportunist policy of all struggle and no alliance. Our Party summed up the lessons of the Right and "Left" opportunist errors and formulated the policy of both alliance and struggle.

Our Party made a series of adjustments in its policies in

order to unite all the anti-Japanese parties and groups, including the Kuomintang, and all the anti-Japanese strata in a joint fight against the foe. We pledged ourselves to fight for the complete realization of Dr. Sun Yat-sen's revolutionary Three People's Principles. The government of the Shensi-Kansu-Ningsia revolutionary base area was renamed the Government of the Shensi-Kansu-Ningsia Special Region of the Republic of China. Our Workers' and Peasants' Red Army was redesignated the Eighth Route Army and the New Fourth Army of the National Revolutionary Army. Our land policy, the policy of confiscating the land of the landlords, was changed to one of reducing rent and interest. In our own base areas we carried out the "three thirds system"[1] in our organs of political power, drawing in those representatives of the petty bourgeoisie, the national bourgeoisie and the enlightened gentry and those members of the Kuomintang who stood for resistance to Japan and did not oppose the Communist Party. In accordance with the principles of the Anti-Japanese National United Front, we also made necessary and appropriate changes in our policies relating to the economy, taxation, labour and wages, anti-espionage, people's rights, culture and education, etc.

While making these policy adjustments, we maintained the independence of the Communist Party, the people's army and the base areas. We also insisted that the Kuomintang should institute a general mobilization, reform the government apparatus, introduce democracy, improve the people's livelihood, arm the people, and carry out a total war of resistance. We waged a resolute struggle against the Kuomintang's passive resistance to Japan and active opposition to the Communist Party, against its suppression of the people's resistance movement and its treacherous activities for compromise and capitulation.

Past experience has taught us that "Left" errors were liable to crop up after our Party had corrected Right errors, and that Right errors were liable to crop up after it had corrected "Left" errors. "Left" errors were liable to occur when we broke

18

with the Kuomintang ruling clique, and Right errors were liable to occur when we united with it.

After the overcoming of "Left" opportunism and the formation of the Anti-Japanese National United Front, the main danger in our Party was Right opportunism or capitulationism.

Wang Ming, the exponent of "Left" opportunism during the Second Revolutionary Civil War, went to the other extreme in the early days of the War of Resistance Against Japan and became the exponent of Right opportunism, *i.e.*, capitulationism. He countered Comrade Mao Tse-tung's correct line and policies with an out-and-out capitulationist line of his own and a series of ultra-Right policies. He voluntarily abandoned proletarian leadership in the Anti-Japanese National United Front and willingly handed leadership to the Kuomintang. By his advocacy of "everything through the united front" or "everything to be submitted to the united front", he was in effect advocating that everything should go through or be submitted to Chiang Kai-shek and the Kuomintang. He opposed the bold mobilization of the masses, the carrying out of democratic reforms and the improvement of the livelihood of the workers and peasants, and wanted to undermine the worker-peasant alliance which was the foundation of the united front. He did not want the Communist-led base areas of the people's revolutionary forces but wanted to cut off the people's revolutionary forces from their roots. He rejected the people's army led by the Communist Party and wanted to hand over the people's armed forces to Chiang Kai-shek, which would have meant handing over everything the people had. He did not want the leadership of the Party and advocated an alliance between the youth of the Kuomintang and that of the Communist Party to suit Chiang Kai-shek's design of corroding the Communist Party. He decked himself out and presented himself to Chiang Kai-shek, hoping to be given some official appointment. All this was revisionism, pure and simple. If we had acted on Wang Ming's revisionist line and his set of policies, the Chinese people would have been unable to win the War of Resistance

Against Japan, still less subsequent nation-wide victory.

For a time during the War of Resistance, Wang Ming,s revisionist line caused harm to the Chinese people's revolutionary cause. But the leading role of Comrade Mao Tse-tung had already been established in the Central Committee of our Party. Under his leadership, all the Marxist-Leninists in the Party carried out a resolute struggle against Wang Ming's errors and rectified them in time. It was this struggle that prevented Wang Ming's erroneous line from doing greater and more lasting damage to the cause of the Party.

Chiang Kai-shek, our teacher by negative example, helped us to correct Wang Ming's mistakes. He repeatedly lectured us with cannons and machine-guns. The gravest lesson was the Southern Anhwei Incident which took place in January 1941. Because some leaders of the New Fourth Army disobeyed the directives of the Central Committee of the Party and followed Wang Ming's revisionist line, its units in southern Anhwei suffered disastrous losses in the surprise attack launched by Chiang Kai-shek and many heroic revolutionary fighters were slaughtered by the Kuomintang revolutionaries. The lessons learned at the cost of blood helped to sober many of our comrades and increase their ability to distinguish the correct from the erroneous line.

Comrade Mao Tse-tung constantly summed up the experience gained by the whole Party in implementing the line of the Anti-Japanese National United Front and worked out a whole set of policies in good time. They were mainly as follows:

1. All people favouring resistance (that is, all the anti-Japanese workers, peasants, soldiers, students and intellectuals, and businessmen) were to unite and form the Anti-Japanese National United Front.

2. Within the united front, our policy was to be one of

independence and initiative, *i.e.*, both unity and independence were necessary.

3. As far as military strategy was concerned, our policy was to be guerrilla warfare waged independently and with the initiative in our own hands, within the framework of a unified strategy; guerrilla warfare was to be basic, but no chance of waging mobile warfare was to be lost when the conditions were favourable.

4. In the struggle against the anti-Communist die-hards headed by Chiang Kai-shek, our policy was to make use of contradictions, win over the many, oppose the few and destroy our enemies one by one, and to wage struggles on just grounds, to our advantage, and with restraint.

5. In the Japanese-occupied with Kuomintang areas our policy was, on the one hand, to develop the united front to the greatest possible extent and, on the other, to have selected cadres working underground. With regard to the forms of organization and struggle, our policy was to assign selected cadres to work under cover for a long period, so as to accumulate strength and bide our time.

6. As regards the alignment of the various classes within the country, our basic policy was to develop the progressive forces, win over the middle forces and isolate the anti-Communist die-hard forces.

7. As for the anti-Communist die-hards, we followed a revolutionary dual policy of uniting with them, in so far as they were still capable of bringing themselves to resist Japan, and of struggling against and isolating them, in so far as they were determined to oppose the Communist Party.

8. With respect to the landlords and the bourgeoisie — even the big landlords and big bourgeoisie — it was necessary to analyse each case and draw distinctions. On the basis of these distinctions we were to formulate different policies so as to achieve our aim of uniting with all the forces that could be

united.

The line and the various policies of the Anti-Japanese National United Front formulated by Comrade Mao Tse-tung stood the test of the War of Resistance and proved to be entirely correct.

History shows that when confronted by ruthless imperialist aggression, a Communist Party must hold aloft the national banner and, using the weapon of the united front, rally around itself the masses and the patriotic and anti-imperialist people who form more than 90 per cent of a country's population, so as to mobilize all positive factors, unite with all the forces that can be united and isolate to the maximum the common enemy of the whole nation. If we abandon the national banner, adopt a line of "closed-doorism" and thus isolate ourselves, it is out of the question to exercise leadership and develop the people's revolutionary cause, and this in reality amounts to helping the enemy and bringing defeat on ourselves.

History shows that within the united front the Communist Party must maintain its ideological, political and organizational independence, adhere to the principle of independence and initiative, and insist on its leading role. Since there are class differences among the various classes in the united front, the Party must have a correct policy in order to develop the progressive forces, win over the middle forces and oppose the die-hard forces. The Party's work must centre on developing the progressive forces and expanding the people's revolutionary forces. This is the only way to maintain and strengthen the united front. "If unity is sought through struggle, it will live; if unity is sought through yielding, it will perish."[2] This is the chief experience gained in our struggle against the die-hard forces.

History shows that during the national-democratic revolution there must be two kinds of alliance within this united front, first, the worker-peasant alliance and, second, the alliance of the working people with the bourgeoisie and other non-working people. The worker-peasant alliance is an alliance of the working class with the peasants and all other working people in town and country. It is the foundation of the united front. Whether the working class can gain leadership of the national-democratic revolution depends on whether it can lead the broad masses of the peasants in struggle and rally them around itself. Only when the working class gains leadership of the peasants, and only on the basis of worker-peasant alliance, is it possible to establish the second alliance, form a broad united front and wage a people's war victoriously. Otherwise, everything that is done is unreliable, like castles in the air or so much empty talk.

1. The "three thirds system" refers to the organs of the political power which were established according to the principle of the Anti-Japanese National United Front and in which the members of the Communist Party, non-Party progressives and the middle elements each occupied one-third of the places.

2. Mao Tse-tung, "Current Problems of Tactics in the Anti-Japanese United Front", *Selected Works*, Eng. Ed., FLP, Peking, 1965, Vol. II, p. 422.

Rely on the Peasants and Establish Rural Base Areas

The peasantry constituted more than 80 per cent of the entire population of semi-colonial and semi-feudal China. They were subjected to the threefold oppression and exploitation of imperialism, feudalism and bureaucrat-capitalism, and they were eager for resistance against Japan for revolution. It was essential to rely mainly on the peasants if the people's war was to be won.

But at the outset not all comrades in our Party saw this point. The history of our Party shows that in the period of the First Revolutionary Civil War, one of the major errors of the

Right opportunists, represented by Chen Tu-hsiu, was their failure to recognize the importance of the peasant question and their opposition to arousing and arming the peasants. In the period of the Second Revolutionary Civil War, one of the major errors of the "Left" opportunists, represented by Wang Ming, was likewise their failure to recognize the importance of the peasant question. They did not realize that it was essential to undertake long-term and painstaking work among the peasants and establish revolutionary base areas in the countryside; they were under the illusion that they could rapidly seize the big cities and quickly win nation-wide victory in the revolution. The errors of both the Right and the "Left" opportunists brought serious setbacks and defeats to the Chinese revolution.

As far back as the period of the First Revolutionary Civil War, Comrade Mao Tse-tung had pointed out that the peasant question occupied an extremely important position in the Chinese revolution, that the bourgeois-democratic revolution against imperialism and feudalism as in essence a peasant revolution and that the basic task of the Chinese proletariat in the bourgeois-democratic revolution was to give leadership to the peasants' struggle.

In the period of the War of Resistance Against Japan, Comrade Mao Tse-tung again stressed that the peasants were the most reliable and the most numerous ally of the proletariat and constituted the main force in the War of Resistance. The peasants were the main source of manpower for China's armies. The funds and the supplies needed for a protracted war came chiefly from the peasants. In the anti-Japanese war it was imperative to rely mainly on the peasants and to arouse them to participate in the war on the broadest scale.

The War of Resistance Against Japan was in essence a peasant revolutionary war led by our Party. By arousing and organizing the peasant masses and integrating them with the proletariat, our Party created a powerful force capable of defeating the strongest enemy.

To rely on the peasants, build rural base areas and use the countryside to encircle and finally capture the cities — such was the way to victory in the Chinese revolution.

Basing himself on the characteristics of the Chinese revolution, Comrade Mao Tse-tung pointed out the importance of building rural revolutionary base areas.

Since China's key cities have long been occupied by the powerful imperialists and their reactionary Chinese allies, it is imperative for the revolutionary ranks to turn the backward villages into advanced, consolidated base areas, into great military, political, economic and cultural bastions of the revolution from which to fight their vicious enemies who are using the cities for attacks on the rural districts, and in this way gradually to achieve the complete victory of the revolution through protracted fighting; it is imperative for them to do so if they do not wish to compromise with imperialism and its lackeys but are determined to fight on, and if they intend to build up and temper their forces, and avoid decisive battles with a powerful enemy while their own strength is inadequate.[1]

Experience in the period of the Second Revolutionary Civil War showed that, when this strategic concept of Comrade Mao Tse-tung's was applied, there was an immense growth in the revolutionary forces and one Red base area after another was built. Conversely, when it was violated and the nonsense of the "Left" opportunists was applied, the revolutionary forces suffered severe damage, with losses of nearly 100 per cent in the cities and 90 per cent in the rural areas.

During the War of Resistance Against Japan, the Japanese imperialist forces occupied many of China's big cities and the main lines of communication, but owing to the shortage of troops they were unable to occupy the vast countryside, which remained the vulnerable sector of the enemy's rule. Consequently, the possibility of building rural base areas became even greater. Shortly after the beginning of the War of Resistance, when the Japanese forces surged into China's hinterland and the Kuomintang forces crumbled and fled in one defeat after another, the Eighth Route and New Fourth Armies led by our Party followed the wise policy laid down by Comrade Mao Tse-tung and boldly drove into the areas behind the enemy lines in small contingents and established base areas throughout the countryside. During the eight years of the war, we established nineteen anti-Japanese base areas in northern, central and southern China. With the exception of the big cities and the main lines of communication, the vast territory in the enemy's rear was in the hands of the people.

In the anti-Japanese base areas, we carried our democratic reforms, improved the livelihood of the people, and mobilized and organized the peasant masses. Organs of anti-Japanese democratic political power were established on an extensive scale and the masses of the people enjoyed the democratic right to run their own affairs; at the same time we carried out the policies of "a reasonable burden" and "the reduction of rent and interest", which weakened the feudal system of exploitation and improved the people's livelihood. As a result, the enthusiasm of the peasant masses was deeply aroused, while the various anti-Japanese strata were given due consideration and were thus united. In formulating our policies for the base areas, we also took care that these policies should facilitate our work in the enemy-occupied areas.

In the enemy-occupied cities and villages, we combined legal with illegal struggle, united the basic masses and all patriots, and divided and disintegrated the political power of the enemy and his puppets so as to prepare ourselves to attack the enemy from within in co-ordination with operations from without when conditions were ripe.

The base areas established by our Party became the centre of gravity in the Chinese people's struggle to resist Japan and save the country. Relying on these bases, our Party expanded and strengthened the people's revolutionary forces, persevered in the protracted war and eventually won the War or

Resistance Against Japan.

Naturally, it was impossible for the development of the revolutionary base areas to be plain sailing all the time. They constituted a tremendous threat to the enemy and were bound to be attacked. Therefore, their development was a tortuous process of expansion, contraction and then renewed expansion. Between 1937 and 1940 the population in the anti-Japanese base areas grew to 100,000,000. But in 1941-42 the Japanese imperialists used the major part of their invading forces to launch frantic attacks on our base areas and wrought havoc. Meanwhile, the Kuomintang, too, encircled these base areas, blockaded them and went so far as to attack them. So by 1942, the anti-Japanese base areas had contracted and their population was less than 50,000,000. Placing complete reliance on the masses, our Party resolutely adopted a series of correct policies and measures, with the result that the base areas were able to hold out under extremely difficult circumstances. After this setback, the army and the people in the base areas were tempered and grew stronger. From 1943 onwards, our base areas were gradually restored and expanded, and by 1945 the population had grown to 160,000,000. Taking the entire course of the Chinese revolution into account, our revolutionary base areas went through even more ups and downs, and they weathered a great many tests before the small, separate base areas, expanding in a series of waves, gradually developed into extensive and contiguous base areas.

At the same time, the work of building the revolutionary base areas was a grand rehearsal in preparation for nation-wide victory. In these base areas, we built the Party, ran the organs of state power, built the people's armed forces and set up mass organizations; we engaged in industry and agriculture and operated cultural, educational and all other undertakings necessary for the independent existence of a separate region. Our base areas were in fact a state in miniature. And with the steady expansion of our work in the base areas, our Party established a powerful people's army, trained cadres for various kinds of work, accumulated experience in many fields and build up both the material and the moral strength that provided favourable conditions for nation-wide victory.

The revolutionary base areas established in the War of Resistance later became the springboards for the People's War of Liberation, in which the Chinese people defeated the Kuomintang reactionaries. In the War of Liberation we continued the policy of first encircling the cities from the countryside and then capturing the cities, and thus won nation-wide victory.

1. Mao Tse-tung, "The Chinese Revolution and the Chinese Communist Party", *Selected Works*, Eng. ed., FLP, Peking, 1965, Vol. II, pp. 316-17.

Build a People's Army of a New Type

"Without a people's army the people have nothing."[1] This is the conclusion drawn by Comrade Mao Tse-tung from the Chinese people's experience in their long years of revolutionary struggle, experience that was bought in blood. This is a universal truth of Marxism-Leninism.

The special feature of the Chinese revolution was armed revolution against armed counter-revolution. The main form of struggle was war and the main form of organization was the army which was under the absolute leadership of the Chinese Communist Party, while all the other forms of organization and struggle led by our Party were co-ordinated, directly or indirectly, with the war.

During the First Revolutionary Civil War, many fine Party comrades took an active part in the armed revolutionary struggle. But our Party was then still in its infancy and did not have a clear understanding of this special feature of the Chinese revolution. It was only after the First Revolutionary Civil War, only after the Kuomintang had betrayed the revolution, massacred large numbers of Communists and destroyed all the revolutionary mass organizations, that our Party reached a clearer understanding of the supreme importance of organizing revolutionary armed forces and of studying the strategy and tactics of revolutionary war, and created the Workers' and Peasants' Red Army, the first people's army under the leadership of the Communist Party of China.

During the Second Revolutionary Civil War, the Workers' and Peasants' Red Army created by Comrade Mao Tse-tung grew considerably and at one time reached a total of 300,000 men. But it later lost nine-tenths of its forces as a result of the wrong political and military lines followed by the "Left" opportunist leadership.

At the start of the War of Resistance Against Japan, the people's army led by the Chinese Communist Party had only a little over 40,000 men. The Kuomintang reactionaries attempted to restrict, weaken and destroy this people's army in every conceivable way. Comrade Mao Tse-tung pointed out that, in these circumstances, in order to sustain the War of Resistance and defeat the Japanese aggressors, it was imperative greatly to expand and consolidate the Eighth Route and New Fourth Armies and all the guerrilla units led by our Party. The whole Party should give close attention to war and study military affairs. Every Party member should be ready at all times to take up arms and go to the front.

Comrade Mao Tse-tung also incisively stated that Communists do not fight for personal military power but must fight for military power for the Party and for the people.

Guided by the Party's correct line of expanding the revolutionary armed forces, the Communist-led Eighth Route and New Fourth Armies and anti-Japanese guerrilla units promptly went to the forefront at the very beginning of the war. We spread the seeds of the people's armed forces in the vast areas behind the enemy lines and kindled the flames of guerrilla warfare everywhere. Our people's army steadily expanded in the struggle, so that by the end of the war it was already a million strong, and there was also a militia of over two million. That was why we were able to engage nearly two-thirds of the Japanese forces of aggression and 95 per cent of the puppet troops and to become the main force in the War of Resistance Against Japan. While resisting the Japanese invading forces, we repulsed three large-scale anti-Communist onslaughts launched by the Kuomintang reactionaries in 1939, 1941 and 1943, and smashed their countless "friction-mongering" activities.

Why were the Eighth Route and New Fourth Armies able to grow big and strong from being small and weak and to score such great victories in the War of Resistance Against Japan?

The fundamental reason was that the Eighth Route and New Fourth Armies were founded on Comrade Mao Tse-tung's theory of army building. They were armies of a new type, a people's army which whole-heartedly serves the interests of the people.

Guided by Comrade Mao Tse-tung's theory on building a people's army, our army was under the absolute leadership of the Chinese Communist Party and most loyally carried out the Party's Marxist-Leninist line and policies. It had a high degree of conscious discipline and was heroically inspired to destroy all enemies and conquer all difficulties. Internally there was full unity between cadres and fighters, between those in higher and those in lower positions of responsibility, between the different departments and between the various fraternal army units. Externally, there was similarly full unity between the army and the people and between the army and the local government.

During the anti-Japanese war our army staunchly performed the three tasks set by Comrade Mao Tse-tung, namely, fighting, mass work, and production, and it was at the same time a fighting force, a political work force and a production corps. Everywhere it went, it did propaganda work among the masses, organized and armed them and helped them set up revolutionary political power. Our armymen strictly observed the Three Main Rules of Discipline and the Eight Points for Attention,[2] carried out campaigns to "support the government and cherish the people", and did good deeds for the people everywhere. They also made use of every possibility to engage in production themselves so as to overcome economic difficulties, better their own livelihood and lighten the people's burden. By their exemplary conduct they won the whole-hearted support of the masses, who affectionately called them "our own boys".

Our army consisted of local forces as well as of regular forces; moreover, it energetically built and developed the militia, thus practising the system of combining the three military formations, *i.e.*, the regular forces, the local forces and the militia.

Our army also pursued correct policies in winning over enemy officers and men in giving lenient treatment to prisoners of war. During the anti-Japanese war we not only brought about the revolt and surrender of large numbers of puppet troops, but succeeded in converting not a few Japanese prisoners, who had been badly poisoned by fascist ideology. After they were politically awakened, they organized themselves into anti-war organizations such as the League for the Liberation of the Japanese People, the Anti-War League of the Japanese in China and the League of Awakened Japanese, helped us to disintegrate the Japanese army and co-operated with us in opposing Japanese militarism. Comrade Sanzo Nosaka, the leader of the Japanese Communist Party, who was then in Yenan, gave us great help in this work.

The essence of Comrade Mao Tse-tung's theory of army building is that in building a people's army prominence must be given to politics, *i.e.*, the army must first and foremost be built on a political basis. Politics is the commander, politics is the soul of everything. Political work is the lifeline of our army. True, a people's army must pay attention to the constant improvement of its weapons and equipment and its military technique, but in its fighting it does not rely purely on weapons and technique, it relies mainly on politics, on the proletarian revolutionary consciousness and courage of the commanders and fighters, on the support and backing of the masses.

Owing to the application of Comrade Mao Tse-tung's line on army building, there has prevailed in our army at all times a high level of proletarian political consciousness, an atmosphere of keenness to study the thought of Mao Tse-tung, an excellent morale, a solid unity and a deep hatred for the enemy, and thus a gigantic moral force has been brought into being. In battle it has feared neither hardships nor death, it has been able to charge or hold its ground as the conditions require. One man can play the role of several, dozens or even hundreds, and miracles can be performed.

All this makes the people's army led by the Chinese Communist Party fundamentally different from any bourgeois army, and from all the armies of the old type which served the exploiting classes and were driven and utilized by a handful of people. The experience of the people's war in China shows that a people's army created in accordance with Comrade Mao Tse-tung's theory of army building is incomparably strong and invincible.

1. Mao Tse-tung, "On Coalition Government", *Selected Works*, Eng. ed., FLP, Peking, 1965, Vol. III, pp. 296-97.

2. The Three Main Rules of Discipline and the Eight Points for Attention were drawn up by Comrade Mao Tse-tung for the Chinese Workers' and Peasants' Red Army during the Agrarian Revolutionary War and were later adopted as rules of discipline by the Eighth Route Army and the New Fourth Army and the present People's Liberation Army. As these rules varied slightly in content in the army units of different areas, the General Headquarters of the Chinese People's Liberation Army in October 1947 issued a standard version as follows:

The Three Main Rules of Discipline:

(1) Obey orders in all your actions.
(2) Do not take a single needle or piece of thread from the masses.
(3) Turn in everything captured.

The Eight Points For Attention:

(1) Speak politely.
(2) Pay fairly for what you buy.
(3) Return everything you borrow.
(4) Pay for anything you damage.
(5) Do not hit or swear at people.
(6) Do not damage crops.
(7) Do not take liberties with women.
(8) Do not ill-treat captives.

Carry out the Strategy and Tactics of People's War

Engels said, "The emancipation of the proletariat, in its turn, will have its specific expression in military affairs and create its specific, new military method." 1936 [1] Engels' profound prediction has been fulfilled in the revolutionary wars waged by the Chinese people under the leadership of the Chinese Communist Party. In the course of protracted armed struggle, we have created a whole range of strategy and tactics of people's war by which we have been able to utilize our strong points to attack the enemy at his weak points.

During the War of Resistance Against Japan, on the basis of his comprehensive analysis of the enemy and ourselves, Comrade Mao Tse-tung laid down the following strategic principle for the Communist-led Eighth Route and New Fourth Armies: "Guerrilla warfare is basic, but lose no chance for mobile warfare under favourable conditions."[2] He raised guerrilla warfare to the level of strategy, because, if they are to defeat a formidable enemy, revolutionary armed forces should not fight with a reckless disregard for the consequences when there is a great disparity between their own strength and their enemy's. If they do, they will suffer serious losses and bring heavy setbacks to the revolution. Guerrilla warfare is the only way to mobilize and apply the whole strength of the people against the enemy, the only way to expand our forces in the course of the war, deplete and weaken the enemy, gradually change the balance of forces between the enemy and ourselves, switch from guerrilla to mobile warfare, and finally defeat the enemy.

In the initial period of the Second Revolutionary Civil War, Comrade Mao Tse-tung enumerated the basic tactics of guerrilla warfare as follows:

The enemy advances, we retreat; the enemy camps, we harass; the enemy tires, we attack; the enemy retreats, we pursue.[3]

Guerrilla war tactics were further developed during the War of Resistance Against Japan. In the base areas behind the enemy lines, everybody joined the fighting — the troops and the civilian population, men and women, old and young; every single village fought. Various ingenious methods of fighting were devised, including "sparrow warfare",[4] land-mine warfare, tunnel warfare, sabotage warfare, and guerrilla warfare on lakes and rivers.

In the later period of the War of Resistance Against Japan and during the Third Revolutionary Civil War, we switched our strategy from that of guerrilla warfare was the primary form of fighting to that of mobile warfare in the light of the changes in the balance of forces between the enemy and ourselves. By the middle, and especially the later, period of the Third Revolutionary Civil War, our operations had developed into large-scale mobile warfare, including the storming of big cities.

War of annihilation is the fundamental guiding principle of our military operations. This guiding principle should be put into effect regardless of whether mobile or guerrilla warfare is the primary form of fighting. It is true that in guerrilla warfare much should be done to disrupt and harass the enemy, but it is still necessary actively to advocate and fight battles of annihilation whenever conditions are favourable. In mobile warfare superior forces must be concentrated in every battle so that the enemy forces can be wiped out one by one. Comrade Mao Tse-tung has pointed out:

A battle in which the enemy is routed is not basically decisive in a contest with a foe of great strength. A battle of annihilation, on the other hand, produces a great and immediate impact on any enemy. Injuring all of a man's ten fingers is not as effective as chopping off one, and routing ten enemy divisions is not as effective as annihilating one of them.[5]

Battles of annihilation are the most effective way of hitting the enemy; each time one of his brigades or regiments is wiped out, he will have one brigade or regiment less, and the enemy forces will be demoralized and will disintegrate. By fighting battles of annihilation, our army is able to take prisoners of war or capture weapons from the enemy in every battle, and the morale of our army rises, our army units get bigger, our weapons become better, and our combat effectiveness continually increases.

In his celebrated ten cardinal military principles Comrade Mao Tse-tung pointed out:

In every battle, concentrate an absolutely superior force (two, three, four and sometimes even five or six times the enemy's strength), encircle the enemy forces completely, strive to wipe them out thoroughly and do not let any escape from the net. In special circumstances, use the method of dealing crushing blows to the enemy, that is, concentrate all our strength to make a frontal attack and also to attack one or both of his flanks, with the aim of wiping out one part and routing another so that our army can swiftly move its troops to smash other enemy forces. Strive to avoid battles of attrition in which we lose more than we gain or only break even. In this way, although we are inferior as a whole (in terms of numbers), we are absolutely superior in every part and every specific campaign, and this ensures victory in the campaign. As time goes on, we shall become superior as a whole and eventually wipe out all the enemy.[6]

At the same time, he said that we should first attack dispersed or isolated enemy forces and only attack concentrated and strong enemy forces later; that we should strive to wipe out the enemy through mobile warfare; that we should fight no battle unprepared and fight no battle we are not sure of winning; and that in any battle we fight we should develop our army's strong points and its excellent style of fighting. These are the major principles of fighting a war of annihilation.

In order to annihilate the enemy, we must adopt the policy of luring him in deep and abandon some cities and districts of our own accord in a planned way, so as to let him in. It is only after letting the enemy in that the people can take part in the war in various ways and that the power of a people's war can be fully exerted. It is only after letting the enemy in that we can be compelled to divide up his forces, take on heavy burdens and commit mistakes. In other words, we must let the enemy become elated, stretch out all his ten fingers and become hopelessly bogged down. Thus, we can concentrate superior forces to destroy the enemy forces one by one, to eat them up mouthful by mouthful. Only by wiping out the enemy's effective strength can cities or localities be finally held or seized. We are firmly against dividing up our forces to defend all positions and putting up resistance at every place for fear that our territory might be lost and our pots and pans smashed, since this can neither wipe out the enemy forces nor hold cities or localities.

Comrade Mao Tse-tung has provided a masterly summary of the strategy and tactics of people's war: You fight in your way and we fight in ours; we fight when we can win and move away when we can't.

In other words, you rely on modern weapons and we rely on highly conscious revolutionary people; you give full play to your superiority and we give full play to ours; you have your way of fighting and we have ours. When you want to fight us, we don't let you and you can't even find us. But when we want to fight you, we make sure that you can't get away and we hit you squarely on the chin and wipe you out. When we are able to wipe you out, we do so with a vengeance; when we can't, we see to it that you don't wipe us out. It is opportunism if one won't fight when one can win. It is adventurism if one insists on fighting when one can't win. Fighting is the pivot of al our strategy and tactics. It is because of the necessity of fighting that we admit the necessity of moving away. The sole purpose of moving away is to fight and bring about the final and complete destruction of the enemy. This strategy and these tactics can be applied only when one relies on the broad masses of the people, and such application brings the superiority of people's war into full play. However superior he may be in technical equipment and whatever tricks he may resort to, the enemy will find himself in the passive position of having to receive blows, and the initiative will always be in our hands.

We grew from a small and weak to a large and strong force and finally defeated formidable enemies at home and abroad because we carried out the strategy and tactics of people's war. During the eight years of War of Resistance Against Japan, the people's army led by the Chinese Communist Party fought more than 125,000 engagements with the enemy and put out of action more than 1,700,000 Japanese and puppet troops. In the three years of the War of Liberation, we put eight million of the Kuomintang's reactionary troops out of action and won the great victory of the people

1. Frederick Engels, "Possibilities and Perspectives of the War of the Holy Alliance Against France in 1852", *Collected Works of Marx and Engels*, Russ. ed., Moscow, 1956, Vol. VII, p. 509.

2. Mao Tse-tung, "On Protracted War", *Selected Works*, Eng. ed., FLP,

Peking, 1965, Vol. II, p. 116.}

3. Mao Tse-tung, "A Single Spark Can Start a Prairie Fire", *Selected Works*, Eng. ed., FLP, Peking, 1965, Vol. I, p. 124.

4. Sparrow warfare is a popular method of fighting created by the Communist-led anti-Japanese guerrilla units and militia behind the enemy lines. It was called sparrow warfare because, first, it was used diffusely, like the flight of sparrows in the sky; and because, second, it was used flexibly by guerrillas or militiamen, operating in threes or fives, appearing and disappearing unexpectedly and wounding, killing, depleting and wearing out the enemy forces.

5. Mao Tse-tung, "Problems of Strategy in China's Revolutionary War", *Selected Works*, Eng. ed., FLP, Peking, 1965, Vol. I, p. 248.

6. Mao Tse-tung, "The Present Situation and Our Tasks", *Selected Works*, Eng. ed., FLP, Peking, 1961j, Vol. IV, p. 161.

Adhere to the Policy of Self-Reliance

The Chinese people's War of Resistance Against Japan was an important part of the Anti-Fascist World War. The victory of the Anti-Fascist War as a whole was the result of the common struggle of the people of the world. By its participation in the war against Japan at the final stage, the Soviet army under the leadership of the Communist Party of the Soviet Union headed by Stalin played a significant part in bringing about the defeat of Japanese imperialism. Great contributions were made by the peoples of Korea, Vietnam, Mongolia, Laos, Cambodia, Indonesia, Burma, India, Pakistan, Malaya, the Philippines, Thailand and certain other Asian countries. The people of the Americas, Oceania, Europe and Africa also made their contribution.

Under extremely difficult circumstances, the Communist Party of Japan and the revolutionary forces of the Japanese people kept up their valiant and staunch struggle, and played their part in the defeat of Japanese fascism.

The common victory was won by all the peoples, who gave one another support and encouragement. Yet each country was, above all, liberated as a result of its own people's efforts.

The Chinese people enjoyed the support of other peoples in winning both the War of Resistance Against Japan and the People's Liberation War, and yet victory was mainly the result of the Chinese people's own efforts. Certain people assert that China's victory in the War of Resistance was due entirely to foreign assistance. This absurd assertion is in tune with that of the Japanese militarists.

The liberation of the masses is accomplished by the masses themselves — this is a basic principle of Marxism-Leninism. Revolution or people's war in any country is the business of the masses in that country and should be carried out primarily by their own efforts; there is no other way.

During the War of Resistance Against Japan, our Party maintained that China should rely mainly on her own strength while at the same time trying to get as much foreign assistance as possible. We firmly opposed the Kuomintang ruling clique's policy of exclusive reliance on foreign aid. In the eyes of the Kuomintang and Chiang Kai-shek, China's industry and agriculture were no good, her weapons and equipment were no good, nothing in China was any good, so that if she wanted to defeat Japan, she had to depend on other countries, and particularly on the U.S.-British imperialists. This was completely slavish thinking. Our policy was diametrically opposed to that of the Kuomintang. Our Party held that it was possible to exploit the contradictions between U.S.-British imperialism and Japanese imperialism, but that no reliance could be placed on the former. In fact, the U.S-British imperialists repeatedly plotted to bring about a "Far Eastern Munich" in order to arrive at a compromise with Japanese imperialism at China's expense, and for a considerable period of time they provided the Japanese aggressors with war *materiél*. In helping China during that period, the U.S. imperialists harboured the sinister design of turning China into a colony of their own.

Comrade Mao Tse-tung said: "China has to rely mainly on her own efforts in the War of Resistance."[1] He added, "We hope for foreign aid but cannot be dependent on it; we depend on our own efforts, on the creative power of the whole army and the entire people."[2]

Self-reliance was especially important for the people's armed forces and the Liberated Areas led by our Party.

The Kuomintang government gave the Eighth Route and New Fourth Armies some small allowances in the initial stage of the anti-Japanese war, but gave them not a single penny later. The Liberated Areas faced great difficulties as a result of the Japanese imperialists' savage attacks and brutal "mopping-up" campaigns, of the Kuomintang's military encirclement and economic blockade and of natural calamities. The difficulties were particularly great in the years 1941 and 1942, when we were very short of food and clothing.

What were we to do? Comrade Mao Tse-tung asked: How has mankind managed to keep alive from time immemorial? Has it not been by men using their hands to provide for themselves? Why should we, their latter-day descendants, be devoid of this tiny bit of wisdom? Why can't we use our own hands?

The Central Committee of the Party and Comrade Mao Tse-tung put forward the policies of "ample food and clothing through self-reliance" and "develop the economy and ensure supplies", and he army and the people of the Liberated Areas accordingly launched an extensive production campaign, with the main emphasis on agriculture.

Difficulties are not invincible monsters. If everyone co-operates and fights them, they will be overcome. The Kuomintang reactionaries thought that it could starve us to death by cutting off allowances and imposing an economic blockade, but in fact it helped us by stimulating us to rely on our own efforts to surmount our difficulties. While launching the great campaign for production, we applied the policy of "better troops and simpler administration" and economized in the use of manpower and material resources; thus we not only surmounted the severe material difficulties and successfully met the crisis, but lightened the people's burden, improved their livelihood and laid the material foundations for victory in the anti-Japanese war.

The problem of military equipment was solved mainly by relying on the capture of arms from the enemy, though we did turn out some weapons too. Chiang Kai-shek, the Japanese imperialists and the U.S. imperialists have all been our "chiefs of transportation corps". The arsenals of the imperialists always provide the oppressed peoples and nations with arms.

The peoples armed forces led by our Party independently waged people's war on a large scale and won great victories without any material aid from outside, both during the more than eight years of the anti-Japanese war and during the more than three years of the People's War of Liberation.

Comrade Mao Tse-tung has said that our fundamental policy should rest on the foundation of our own strength. Only by relying on our own efforts can we in all circumstances remain invincible.

The peoples of the world invariably support each other in their struggles against imperialism and its lackeys. Those countries which have won victory are duty bound to support and aid the peoples who have not yet done so. Nevertheless, foreign aid can only play a supplementary role.

In order to fight a revolution and to fight a people's war and be victorious, it is imperative to adhere to the policy of self-reliance, rely on the strength of the masses in one's won country and prepare to carry on the fight independently even when all material aid from outside is cut off. If one does not operate by one's own efforts, does not independently ponder and solve the problems of the revolution in one's own country and does not rely on the strength of the masses, but leans wholly on foreign aid — even though this be aid from socialist countries which persist in revolution — no victory can be won, or be consolidated even if it is won.

1. Mao Tse-tung, "Interview with Three Correspondents from the Central News Agency, the *Sao Tang Pao* and the *Hsin Min Pao* ", *Selected Works*, Eng. ed., FLP, Peking, 1965, Vol. II, p. 270.

2. Mao Tse-tung, "We Must Learn to do Economic Work", *Selected Works*, Eng. ed., FLP, Peking, 1965, Vol. III, p. 241.

The International Significance of Comrade Mao-Tse Tung's Theory of People's War

The Chinese revolution is a continuation of the great October Revolution. The road of the October Revolution is the common road for all people's revolutions. The Chinese revolution and the October Revolution have in common the following basic characteristics: (1) Both were led by the working class with a Marxist-Leninist party as its nucleus. (2) Both were based on the worker-peasant alliance. (3) In both cases state power was seized through violent revolution and the dictatorship of the proletariat was established. (4) In both cases the socialist system was built after victory in the revolution. (5) Both were component parts of the proletarian world revolution.

Naturally, the Chinese revolution had its own peculiar characteristics. The October Revolution took place in imperialist Russia, but the Chinese revolution broke out in a semi-colonial and semi-feudal country. The former was a proletarian socialist revolution, while the latter developed into a socialist revolution after the complete victory of the new-democratic revolution. The October Revolution began with armed uprisings in the cities and then spread to the countryside, while the Chinese revolution won nation-wide victory through the encirclement of the cities from the rural areas and the final capture of the cities.

Comrade Mao Tse-tung's great merit lies in the fact that he has succeeded in integrating the universal truth of Marxism-Leninism with the concrete practice of the Chinese revolution and has enriched and developed Marxism-Leninism by his masterly generalization and summation of the experience gained during the Chinese people's protracted revolutionary struggle.

Comrade Mao Tse-tung's theory of people's war has been proved by the long practice of the Chinese revolution to be in accord with the objective laws of such wars and to be invincible. It has not only been valid for China, it is a great contribution to the revolutionary struggles of the oppressed nations and peoples throughout the world.

The people's war led by the Chinese Communist Party, comprising the War of Resistance and the Revolutionary Civil Wars, lasted for twenty-two years. It constitutes the most drawn-out and most complex people's war led by the proletariat in modern history, and it has been the richest in experience.

In the last analysis, the Marxist-Leninist theory of proletarian revolution is the theory of the seizure of state power by revolutionary violence, the theory of countering war against the people by people's war. As Marx so aptly put it, "Force is the midwife of every old society pregnant with a new one. "[1]

It was on the basis of the lessons derived from the people's wars in China that Comrade Mao Tse-tung, using the simplest and the most vivid language, advanced the famous thesis that "political power grows out of the barrel of a gun".[2]

He clearly pointed out:

The seizure of power by armed force, the settlement of the issue by war, is the central task and the highest form of revolution. This Marxist-Leninist principle of revolution holds good universally, for China and for all other countries. [3]

War is the product of imperialism and the system of exploitation of man by man. Lenin said that "war is always and everywhere begun by the exploiters themselves, by ruling and oppressing classes". [4] So long as imperialism and the system of exploitation of man by man exist, the imperialists and reactionaries will invariably rely on armed force to maintain their reactionary rule and impose war on the oppressed nations and peoples. This is an objective law independent of man's will.

In the world today, all the imperialists headed by the United States and their lackeys, without exception, are strengthening their state machinery, and especially their armed forces. U.S. imperialism, in particular, is carrying out armed aggression and suppression everywhere.

What should the oppressed nations and the oppressed people do in the face of wars of aggression and armed suppression by the imperialists and their lackeys? Should they submit and remain slaves in perpetuity? Or should they rise in resistance and fight for their liberation?

Comrade Mao Tse-tung answered this question in vivid terms. He said that after long investigation and study the Chinese people discovered that all the imperialists and their lackeys "have swords in their hands and are out to kill. The people have come to understand this and so act after the same fashion".[5] This is called doing unto them what they do unto us.

In the last analysis, whether one dares to wage a tit-for-tat struggle against armed aggression and suppression by the imperialists and their lackeys, whether one dares to fight a people's war against them, means whether one dares to embark on revolution. This is the most effective touchstone for distinguishing genuine from fake revolutionaries and Marxist-Leninists.

In view of the fact that some people were afflicted with the fear of the imperialists and reactionaries, Comrade Mao Tse-tung put forward his famous thesis that "the imperialists and all reactionaries are paper tigers". He said,

All reactionaries are paper tigers. In appearance, the reactionaries are terrifying, but in reality they are not so powerful. From a long-term point of view, it is not the reactionaries but the people who are really powerful.[6]

The history of the peoples war in China and other countries provides conclusive evidence that the growth of the people's revolutionary forces from weak and small beginnings into strong and large forces is a universal law of development of people's war. A people's war inevitably meets with many difficulties, with ups and downs and setbacks in the course of its development, but no force can alter its general trend towards inevitable triumph.

Comrade Mao Tse-tung points out that we must despise the enemy strategically and take full account of him tactically.

To despise the enemy strategically is an elementary requirement for a revolutionary. Without the courage to despise the enemy and without daring to win, it will be simply impossible to make revolution and wage a people's war, let alone to achieve victory.

It is also very important for revolutionaries to take full account of the enemy tactically. It is likewise impossible to win victory in a people's war without taking full account of the enemy tactically, and without examining the concrete conditions, without being prudent and giving great attention to the study of the art of struggle, and without adopting appropriate forms of struggle in the concrete practice of the revolution in each country and with regard to each concrete problem of struggle.

Dialectical and historical materialism teaches us that what is important is primarily is not that which at the given moment seems to be durable and yet is already beginning to die away, but that which is arising and developing, even though at the given moment it may not appear to be durable, for only that which is arising and developing is invincible.

Why can the apparently weak new-born forces always triumph over the decadent forces which appear so powerful? The reason is that truth is on their side and that the masses are on their side, while the reactionary classes are always divorced from the masses and set themselves against the masses.

This has been borne out by the victory of the Chinese revolution, by the history of all revolutions, the whole history of class struggle and the entire history of mankind.

The imperialists are extremely afraid of Comrade Mao Tse-tung's thesis that "imperialism and all reactionaries are paper tigers", and the revisionists are extremely hostile to it. They all oppose and attack this thesis and the philistines follow suit by ridiculing it. But all this cannot in the least diminish its importance. The light of truth cannot be dimmed by anybody.

Comrade Mao Tse-tung's theory of people's war solves not only the problem of daring to fight a people's war, but also that of how to wage it.

Comrade Mao Tse-tung is a great statesman and military scientist, proficient at directing war in accordance with its laws. By the line and policies, the strategy and tactics be formulated for people's war, he led the Chinese people in steering the ship of the people's war past all hidden reefs to the shores of victory in most complicated and difficult conditions.

It must be emphasized that Comrade Mao Tse-tung's theory of the establishment of rural revolutionary base areas and the encirclement of the cities from the countryside is of outstanding and universal practical importance for the present revolutionary struggles of all the oppressed nations and peoples, and particularly for the revolutionary struggles of the oppressed nations and peoples in Asia, Africa and Latin America against imperialism and its lackeys.

Many countries and peoples in Asia, Africa and Latin America are now being subjected to aggression and enslavement on a serious scale by the imperialists headed by the United States and their lackeys. The basic political and economic conditions in many of these countries have many similarities to those that prevailed in old China. As in China, the peasant question is extremely important in these regions. The peasants constitute the main force of the national-democratic revolution against the imperialists and their lackeys. In committing aggression against these countries, the imperialists usually begin by seizing the big cities and the main lines of communication, but they are unable to bring the vast countryside completely under their control. The countryside, and the countryside alone, can provide the broad areas in which the revolutionaries can manoeuvre freely. The countryside, and the countryside alone, can provide the revolutionary bases from which the revolutionaries can go forward to final victory. Precisely for this reason, Comrade Mao Tse-tung's theory of establishing revolutionary base areas in the rural districts and encircling the cities from the countryside is attracting more and more attention among the people in these regions.

Taking the entire globe, if North America and Western Europe can be called "the cities of the world", then Asia, Africa and Latin America constitute "the rural areas of the world". Since World War II, the proletarian revolutionary movement has for various reasons been temporarily held back in the North American and West European capitalist countries, while the people's revolutionary movement in Asia, Africa and Latin America has been growing vigorously. In a sense, the contemporary world revolution also presents a picture of the encirclement of cities by the rural areas. In the final analysis, the whole cause of world revolution hinges on the revolutionary struggles of the Asian, African and Latin American peoples who make up the overwhelming majority of the world's population. The socialist countries should regard it as their internationalist duty to support the people's revolutionary struggles in Asia, Africa and Latin America.

The October Revolution opened up a new era in the revolution of the oppressed nations. The victory of the October Revolution built a bridge between the socialist revolution of the proletariat of the West and the national-democratic revolution of the colonial and semi-colonial countries of the East. The Chinese revolution has successfully solved the problem of how to link up the national-democratic with the socialist revolution in the colonial and semi-colonial countries.

Comrade Mao Tse-tung has pointed out that, in the epoch since the October Revolution, anti-imperialist revolution in any colonial or semi-colonial country is no longer part of the old bourgeois, or capitalist world revolution, but is part of the new world revolution, the proletariat-socialist world revolution.

Comrade Mao Tse-tung has formulated a complete theory of the new-democratic revolution. He indicated that this revolution, which is different from all others, can only be, nay must be, a revolution against imperialism, feudalism and bureaucrat-capitalism waged by the broad masses of the people under the leadership of the proletariat.

This means that the revolution can only be, nay must be, led by the proletariat and the genuinely revolutionary party armed with Marxism-Leninism, and by no other class or party.

This means that the revolution embraces in its ranks not only the workers, peasants and the urban petty bourgeoisie, but also the national bourgeoisie and other patriotic and anti-imperialist democrats.

This means, finally, that the revolution is directed against imperialism, feudalism and bureaucrat-capitalism.

The new-democratic revolution leads to socialism, and not to capitalism.

Comrade Mao Tse-tung's theory of the new-democratic revolution is the Marxist-Leninist theory of revolution by stages as well as the Marxist-Leninist theory of uninterrupted revolution.

Comrade Mao Tse-tung made a correct distinction between the two revolutionary stages, *i.e.*, the national-democratic and the socialist revolutions; at the same time he correctly and closely linked the two. The national-democratic revolution is the necessary preparation for the socialist revolution, and the socialist revolution is the inevitable sequel to the national-democratic revolution. There is no Great Wall between the two revolutionary stages. But the socialist revolution is only possible after the completion of the national-democratic revolution. The more thorough the national-democratic revolution, the better the conditions for the socialist revolution.

The experience of the Chinese revolution shows that the tasks of the national-democratic revolution can be fulfilled only through long and tortuous struggles. In this stage of revolution, imperialism and its lackeys are the principal enemy. In the struggle against imperialism and its lackeys, it is necessary to rally all anti-imperialist patriotic forces, including the national bourgeoisie and all patriotic personages. All those patriotic personages from among the bourgeoisie and other exploiting classes who join the anti-imperialist struggle play a progressive historical role; they are not tolerated by imperialism but welcomed by the proletariat.

It is very harmful to confuse the two stages, that is, the national-democratic and the socialist revolutions. Comrade Mao Tse-tung criticized the wrong idea of "accomplishing both at one stroke", and pointed out that this utopian idea could only weaken the struggle against imperialism and its lackeys, the most urgent task at that time. The Kuomintang reactionaries and the Trotskyites they hired during the War of Resistance deliberately confused these two stages of the Chinese revolution, proclaiming the "theory of a single revolution" and preaching so-called "socialism" without any Communist Party, wipe out any revolution and prevent the advance of the national-democratic revolution, and they used it as a pretext for their non-resistance and capitulation to imperialism. This reactionary theory was buried long ago by the history of the Chinese revolution.

The Khrushchov revisionists are now actively preaching that socialism can be built without the proletariat and without a genuinely revolutionary party armed with the advanced proletarian ideology, and they have cast the fundamental tenets of Marxism-Leninism to the four winds. The revisionists' purpose is solely to divert the oppressed nations from their struggle against imperialism and sabotage their national-democratic revolution, all in the service of imperialism.

The Chinese revolution provides a successful lesson for making a thoroughgoing national-democratic revolution under the leadership of the proletariat; it likewise provides a successful lesson for the timely transition from the national-democratic revolution to the socialist revolution under the leadership of the proletariat.

Mao Tse-tung's thought has been the guide to the victory of the Chinese revolution. It has integrated the universal truth of Marxism-Leninism with the concrete practice of the Chinese revolution and creatively developed Marxism-Leninism, thus adding new weapons to the arsenal of Marxism-Leninism.

Ours is the epoch in which world capitalism and imperialism are heading for their doom and socialism and communism are marching to victory. Comrade Mao Tse-tung's theory of people's war is not only a product of the Chinese revolution, but has also the characteristics of our epoch. The new experience gained in the people's revolutionary struggles in various countries since World War II has provided continuous evidence that Mao Tse-tung's thought is a common asset of the revolutionary people of the whole world. This is the great international significance of the thought of Mao Tse-tung.

1. Karl Marx, *Capital*, Eng. ed., Foreign Languages Publishing House, Moscow, 1954, Vol. I, p. 751.

2. Mao Tse-tung, "Problems of War and Strategy", *Selected Works*, Eng. ed., FLP, Peking, 1965, Vol. II, p. 224.

3. *Ibid.*, p. 219.

4. V.I. Lenin, "The Revolutionary Army and the Revolutionary Government", *Collected Works*, Eng. ed., FLPH, Moscow, 1962, Vol. VIII, p. 565.

5. Mao Tse-tung, "The Situation and Our Policy After the Victory in the War of Resistance Against Japan", *Selected Works*, Eng. ed., FLP, Peking, 1961, Vol. IV, pp. 14-15.

6. Mao Tse-tung, "Talk with the American Correspondent Anna Louise Strong", *Selected Works*, Eng. ed., FLP, Peking, 1961, Vol. IV, p. 100.

Defeat U.S. Imperialism and Its Lackeys by People's War

Since World War II, U.S. imperialism has stepped into the shoes of German, Japanese and Italian fascism and has been trying to build a great American empire by dominating and enslaving the whole world. It is actively fostering Japanese and West German militarism as its chief accomplices in unleashing a world war. Like a vicious world, it is bullying and enslaving various peoples, plundering their wealth, encroaching upon their countries' sovereignty and interfering in their internal affairs. It is the most rabid aggressor in human history and the most ferocious common enemy of the people of the world. Every people or country in the world that wants revolution, independence and peace cannot but direct the spearhead of its struggle against U.S. imperialism.

Just as the Japanese imperialists' policy of subjugating China made it possible for the Chinese people to form the broadest possible united front against them, so the U.S. imperialists' policy of seeking world domination makes it possible for the people throughout the world to unite all the forces that can be united and form the broadest possible united front for a converging attack on U.S. imperialism.

At present, the main battlefield of the fierce struggle between the people of the world on one side and U.S. imperialism and its lackeys on the other is the vast area of Asia, Africa and Latin America. In the world as a whole, this is the area where the people suffer worst from imperialist oppression and where imperialist rule is most vulnerable. Since World War II, revolutionary storms have been rising in this area, and today they have become the most important force directly pounding U.S. imperialism. The contradiction between the revolutionary peoples of Asia, Africa and Latin America and the imperialists headed by the United States is the principal contradiction in the contemporary world. The development of this contradiction is promoting the struggle of the people of the whole world against U.S. imperialism and its lackeys.

Since World War II, people's war has increasingly demonstrated its power in Asia, Africa and Latin America. The peoples of China, Korea, Vietnam, Laos, Cuba, Indonesia, Algeria and other countries have waged people's wars against the imperialists and their lackeys and won great victories. The classes leading these people's wars may vary, and so may the breadth and depth of mass mobilization and the extent of victory, but the victories in these people's wars have very much weakened and pinned down the forces of imperialism, upset the U.S. imperialist plan to launch a world war, and become mighty factors defending world peace.

Today, the conditions are more favourable than ever before the waging of people's wars by the revolutionary peoples of Asia, Africa and Latin America against U.S. imperialism and its lackeys.

Since World War II and the succeeding years of revolutionary upsurge, there has been a great rise in the level of political consciousness and the degree of organization of the people in all countries, and the resources available to them for mutual support and aid have greatly increased. The whole capitalist-imperialist system has become drastically weaker and is in the process of increasing convulsion and disintegration. After World War I, the imperialists lacked the power to destroy the new-born socialist Soviet state, but they were still able to suppress the people's revolutionary movements in some countries in the parts of the world under their own rule and so maintain a short period of comparative stability. Since World War II, however, not only have they been unable to stop a number of countries from taking the socialist road, but they are no longer capable of holding back the surging tide of the people's revolutionary movements in the areas under their own rule.

U.S. imperialism is stronger, but also more vulnerable, than any imperialism of the past. It sets itself against the people of the whole world, including the people of the United States. Its human, military, material and financial resources are far from sufficient for the realization of its ambition of dominating the whole world. U.S. imperialism has further weakened itself by occupying so many places in the world, over-reaching itself, stretching its fingers out wide and dispersing its strength, with its rear so far away and its supply lines so long. As Comrade Mao Tse-tung has said, "Wherever it commits aggression, it puts a new noose around its neck. It is besieged ring upon ring by the people of the whole world. "[1]

When committing aggression in a foreign country, U.S. imperialism can only employ part of its forces, which are sent to fight an unjust war far from their native land and therefore have a low morale, and so U.S. imperialism is beset with great difficulties. The people subjected to its aggression are having a trial of strength with U.S. imperialism neither in Washington or New York, neither in Honolulu nor Florida, but are fighting for independence and freedom on their own soil. Once they are mobilized on a broad scale, they will have inexhaustible strength. Thus superiority will belong not to the United States but to the people subjected to its aggression. The latter, though apparently weak and small, are really more powerful than U.S. imperialism.

The struggles waged by the different peoples against U.S. imperialism reinforce each other and merge into a torrential world-wide tide of opposition to U.S. imperialism. The more successful the development of people's war in a given region, the larger the number of U.S. imperialist forces that can be pinned down and depleted there. When the U.S. aggressors are hard pressed in one place, they have no alternative but to loosen their grip on others. Therefore, the conditions become more favourable for the people elsewhere to wage struggles against U.S. imperialism and its lackeys.

Everything is divisible. And so is this colossus of U.S. imperialism. It can be split up and defeated. The peoples of Asia, Africa and Latin America and other regions can destroy it piece by piece, some striking at its head and others at its feet. That is why the greatest fear of U.S. imperialism is that people's wars will be launched in different parts of the world, and particularly in Asia, Africa and Latin America, and why it regards people's war as a mortal danger.

U.S. imperialism relies solely on its nuclear weapons to intimidate people. But these weapons cannot save U.S. imperialism from its doom. Nuclear weapons cannot be used lightly. U.S. imperialism has been condemned by the people of the world for its towering crime of dropping two atom bombs on Japan. If it uses nuclear weapons again, it will become isolated in the extreme. Moreover, the U.S. monopoly of nuclear weapons has long been broken; U.S. imperialism has these weapons, but others have them too. If it threatens other

countries with nuclear weapons, U.S. imperialism will expose its own country to the same threat. For this reason, it will meet with strong opposition not only from the people elsewhere but also inevitably from the people in its own country. Even if U.S. imperialism brazenly uses nuclear weapons, it cannot conquer the people, who are indomitable.

However highly developed modern weapons and technical equipment may be and however complicated the methods of modern warfare, in the final analysis the outcome of a war will be decided by the sustained fighting of the ground forces, by the fighting at close quarters on battlefields, by the political consciousness of the men, by their courage and spirit of sacrifice. Here the weak points of U.S. imperialism will be completely laid bare, while the superiority of the revolutionary people will be brought into full play. The reactionary troops of U.S. imperialism cannot possibly be endowed with the courage and the spirit of sacrifice possessed by the revolutionary people. The spiritual atom bomb which the revolutionary people possess is a far more powerful and useful weapon than the physical atom bomb.

Vietnam is the most convincing current example of a victim of aggression defeating U.S. imperialism by a people's war. The United States has made South Vietnam a testing ground for the suppression of people's war. It has carried on this experiment for many years, and everybody can now see that the U.S. aggressors are unable to find a way of coping with people's war. On the other hand, the Vietnamese people have brought the power of people's war into full play in their struggle against the U.S. aggressors. The U.S. aggressors are in danger of being swamped in the people's war in Vietnam. They are deeply worried that their defeat in Vietnam will lead to a chain reaction. They are expanding the war in an attempt to save themselves from defeat. But the more they expand the war, the greater will be the chain reaction. The more they escalate the war, the heavier will be their fall and the more disastrous their defeat. The people in other parts of the world will see still more clearly that U.S. imperialism can be defeated, and that what the Vietnamese people can do, they can do too.

History has proved and will go on proving that people's war is the most effective weapon against U.S imperialism and its lackeys. All revolutionary people will learn to wage people's war against U.S. imperialism and its lackeys. They will take up arms, learn to fight battles and become skilled in waging people's war, though they have not done so before. U.S. imperialism like a mad bull dashing from place to place, will finally be burned to ashes in the blazing fires of the people's wars it has provoked by its own actions.

1. Mao Tse-tung, Statement Supporting the People of the Congo (Leopoldville) Against U.S. Aggression, November 28, 1964.

The Khrushchev Revisionists are Betrayers of People's War

The Khrushchev revisionists have come to the rescue of U.S. imperialism just when it is most panic-stricken and helpless in its efforts to cope with people's war. Working hand in glove with the U.S. imperialists, they are doing their utmost to spread all kinds of arguments against people's war and, wherever they can, they are scheming to undermine it by overt or covert means.

The fundamental reason why the Khrushchev revisionists are opposed to people's war is that they have no faith in the masses and are afraid of U.S. imperialism, of war and of revolution. Like all other opportunists, they are blind to the power of the masses and do not believe that the revolutionary people are capable of defeating imperialism. They submit to the nuclear blackmail of the U.S. imperialists and are afraid that, if the oppressed peoples and nations rise up to fight people's wars of the people of socialist countries repulse U.S. imperialist aggression, U.S. imperialism will become incensed, they themselves will become involved and their fond dream of Soviet-U.S. co-operation to dominate the world will be spoiled.

Ever since Lenin led the great October Revolution to victory, the experience of innumerable revolutionary wars has borne out the truth that a revolutionary people who rise up with only their bare hands at the outset finally succeed in defeating the ruling classes who are armed to the teeth. The poorly armed have defeated the better armed. People's armed forces, beginning with only primitive swords, spears, rifles and hand-grenades, have in the end defeated the imperialist forces armed with modern aeroplanes, tanks, heavy artillery and atom bombs. Guerrilla forces have ultimately defeated regular armies. "Amateurs" who were never trained in any military schools have eventually defeated "professionals" graduated from military academies. And so on and so forth. Things stubbornly develop in a way that runs counter to the assertions of the revisionists, and facts are slapping them in the face.

The Khrushchev revisionists insist that a nation without nuclear weapons is incapable of defeating an enemy with nuclear weapons, whatever methods of fighting it may adopt. This is tantamount to saying that anyone without nuclear weapons is destined to come to grief, destined to be bullied and annihilated, and must either capitulate to the enemy when confronted with his nuclear weapons or some under the "protection" of some other nuclear power and submit to its beck and call. Isn't this the jungle law of survival par excellence? Isn't this helping the imperialists in their nuclear blackmail? Isn't this openly forbidding people to make revolution?

The Khrushchev revisionists assert that nuclear weapons and strategic rocket units are decisive while conventional forces are insignificant, and that a militia is just a heap of human flesh. For ridiculous reasons such as these, they oppose the mobilization of and reliance on the masses in socialist countries to get prepared to use people's war against imperialist aggression. They have staked the whole future of their country on nuclear weapons and are engaged in a nuclear gamble with U.S. imperialism, with which they are trying to strike a political deal. Their theory of military strategy is the theory that nuclear weapons decide everything. Their line in army building is the bourgeois line which ignores the human factor and sees only the material factor and which regards technique as everything and politics as nothing.

The Khrushchev revisionists maintain that a single spark in any part of the world may touch off a world nuclear conflagration and bring destruction to mankind. If this were true, our planet would have been destroyed time and time again. There have been wars of national liberation throughout the twenty years since World War II. But has any single one of them developed into a world war? Isn't it true that the U.S. imperialists' plans for a world war have been upset precisely thanks to the wars in Asia, Africa, and Latin America? By contrast, those who have done their utmost to stamp out the "sparks" of people's war have in fact encouraged U.S. imperialism in its aggression and wars.

The Khrushchev revisionists claim that if their general line of "peaceful coexistence, peaceful transition and peaceful competition" is followed, the oppressed will be liberated and "a world without weapons, without armed forces and without wars" will come into being. But the inexorable fact is that imperialism and reaction headed by the United States are zealously priming their war machine and are daily engaged in sanguinary suppression of the revolutionary peoples and in the threat and use of armed force against independent forces. The kind of rubbish peddled by the Khrushchev revisionists has already taken a great toll of lives in a number of countries. Are these painful lessons, paid for in blood, still insufficient? The essence of the general line of the Khrushchev revisionists is nothing other than the demand that all the oppressed peoples and nations and all the countries which have won independence should lay down their arms and place themselves at the mercy of the U.S. imperialists and their lackeys who are armed to the teeth.

"While magistrates are allowed to burn down houses, the common people are forbidden even to light lamps. " Such is the way of the imperialists and reactionaries. Subscribing to this imperialist philosophy, the Khrushchev revisionists shout at the Chinese people standing in the forefront of the fight for world peace: "You are bellicose!" Gentlemen, your abuse adds to our credit. It is this very "bellicosity" of ours that helps to prevent imperialism from unleashing a world war. The people are "bellicose" because they have to defend themselves and because the imperialists and reactionaries force them to be so. It is also the imperialists and reactionaries who have taught the people the arts of war. We are simply using revolutionary "bellicosity" to cope with counter-revolutionary bellicosity. How can it be argued that the imperialists and their lackeys may kill people everywhere, while the people must not strike back in self-defence or help one another? What kind of logic is this? The Khrushcheov revisionists regard the imperialists like Kennedy and Johnson as "sensible" and describe us together with all those who dare to carry out armed defence against imperialist aggression as "bellicose". This has revealed the Khrushchev revisionists in their true colours as the accomplices of imperialist gangsters.

We know that war brings destruction, sacrifice and suffering on the people. But the destruction, sacrifice and suffering will be much greater if no resistance is offered to imperialist armed aggression and the people become willing slaves. The sacrifice of a small number of people in revolutionary wars is repaid by security for whole nations, whole countries and even the whole of mankind; temporary suffering is repaid by lasting of even perpetual peace and happiness. War can temper the people and push history forward. In this sense, war is a great school.

When discussing World War I, Lenin said,

> The war has brought hunger to the most civilized
> countries, to those most culturally developed. On the
> other hand, the war, as a tremendous historical process,
> has accelerated social development to an unheard-of
> degree.[1]

He added,

War has shaken up the masses, its untold horrors and
suffering have awakened them. War has given history
momentum and it is now flying with locomotive speed.[2]

If the arguments of the Khrushchov revisionists are to be
believed, would not that make Lenin the worst of all "bellicose
elements"?

In diametrical opposition to the Khrushchov revisionists,
the Marxist-Leninists and revolutionary people never take a
gloomy view of war. Our attitude towards imperialist wars of
aggression has always been clear-cut. First, we are against
them, and secondly, and secondly, we are not afraid of them. We
will destroy whoever attacks us. As for revolutionary wars
waged by the oppressed nations and peoples, so far from
opposing them, we invariably give them firm support and active
aid. It has been so in the past, it remains so in the present and,
when we grow in strength as time goes on, we will give them
still more support and aid in the future. It is sheer day-dreaming
for anyone to think that, since our revolution has been
victorious, our national construction is forging ahead, our
national wealth is increasing and our living conditions are
improving, we too will lose our revolutionary fighting will,
abandon the cause of world revolution and discard Marxism-
Leninism and proletarian internationalism. Of course, every
revolution in a country stems from the demands of its own
people. Only when the people in a country are awakened,

mobilized, organized and armed can they overthrow the reactionary rule of imperialism and its lackeys through struggle; their role cannot be replaced or taken over by any people from outside. In this sense, revolution cannot be imported. But this does not exclude mutual sympathy and support on the part of revolutionary peoples in their struggles against the imperialists and their lackeys. Our support and aid to other revolutionary peoples serves precisely to help their self-reliant struggle.

The propaganda of the Khrushchov revisionists against people's war and the publicity they give to defeatism and capitulationism tend to demoralize and spiritually disarm revolutionary people everywhere. These revisionists are doing what the U.S. imperialists are unable to do themselves and are rendering them great service. They have greatly - encouraged U.S. imperialism in its war adventures. They have completely betrayed the Marxist-Leninist revolutionary theory of war and have become betrayers of people's war.

To win the struggle against U.S. imperialism and carry people's wars to victory, the Marxist-Leninists and revolutionary people throughout the world must resolutely oppose Khrushchov revisionism.

Today, Khrushchov revisionism has a dwindling audience among the revolutionary people of the world. Wherever there is armed aggression and suppression by imperialism and its lackeys, there are bound to be people's wars against aggression and oppression. It is certain that such wars will develop vigorously. This is an objective law independent of the will of either the U.S. imperialists or the Khrushchov revisionists. The revolutionary people of the world will sweep away everything that stands in the way of their advance. Khrushchov is finished. And the successors to Khrushchov revisionism will fare no better. The imperialists, the reactionaries and the Khrushchov revisionists, who have all set themselves against people's war, will be swept like dust from the stage of history by the mighty broom of the revolutionary people.

* * *

Great changes have taken place in China and the world in the twenty years since the victory of the War of Resistance Against Japan, changes that have made the situation more favourable than ever for the revolutionary people of the world and more unfavourable than ever for imperialism and its lackeys.

When Japanese imperialism launched its war of aggression against China, the Chinese people had only a very small people's army and a very small revolutionary base area, and they were up against the biggest military despot of the East. Yet even then, Comrade Mao Tsetung said that the Chinese people's war could be won and that Japanese imperialism could be defeated. Today, the revolutionary base areas of the peoples of the world have grown to unprecedented proportions, their revolutionary movement is surging as never before, imperialism is weaker than ever, and U.S. imperialism, the chieftain of world imperialism, is suffering one defeat after another. We can say with even greater confidence that the people's wars can be won and U.S. imperialism can be defeated in all countries.

The peoples of the world now have the lessons of the October Revolution, the Anti-Fascist War, the Chinese people's War of Resistance and War of Liberation, the Korean people's War of Resistance to U.S. Aggression, the Vietnamese people's War of Liberation and their War of Resistance to U.S. Aggression, and the people's revolutionary armed struggles in many other countries. Provided each people studies these lessons well and creatively integrates them with the concrete practice of revolution in their own country, there is no doubt that the revolutionary peoples of the world will stage still more powerful and splendid dramas in the theatre of people's war in their countries and that they will wipe off the earth once and for all the common enemy of all the people's, U.S. imperialism and its lackeys.

The struggle of the Vietnamese people against U.S. aggression and for natural salvation is now the focus of the struggle of the people of the world against U.S. aggression. The determination of the Chinese people to support and aid the Vietnamese people in their struggle against U.S. aggression and for natural salvation is unshakable. No matter what U.S. imperialism may do to expand its war adventure, the Chinese people will do everything in their power to support the Vietnamese people until every single one of the U.S. aggressors is driven out of Vietnam.

The U.S. imperialists are now clamouring for another trial of strength with the Chinese people, for another large-scale ground war on the Asian mainland. If they insist on following in the footsteps of the Japanese fascists, well then, they may do so, if they please. The Chinese people definitely have ways of their own for coping with a U.S. imperialist war of aggression. Our methods are no secret. The most important one is still mobilization of the people, reliance on the people, making every one a soldier and waging a people's war.

We want to tell the U.S. imperialists once again that the vast ocean of several hundred million Chinese people in arms will be more than enough to submerge your few million aggressor troops. If you dare to impose war on us, we shall gain freedom of action. It will then not be up to you to decide how the war will be fought. We shall fight in the ways most advantageous to us to destroy the enemy and wherever the enemy can be most easily destroyed. Since the Chinese people were able to destroy the Japanese aggressors twenty years ago, they are certainly still more capable finishing off the U.S. aggressors today. The naval and air superiority you boast about cannot intimidate the Chinese people, and neither can the atom bomb you brandish at us. If you want to send troops, go ahead, the more the better. The will annihilate as many as you can send, and can even give you receipts. The Chinese people are a great, valiant people. We have the courage to shoulder the heavy burden of combating U.S. imperialism and to contribute our share in the struggle for final victory over this most ferocious enemy of the people of the world.

It must be pointed out in all seriousness that after the victory of the War of Resistance Taiwan was returned to China. The occupation of Taiwan by U.S. imperialism is absolutely unjustified. Taiwan province is an inalienable part of Chinese territory. The U.S. imperialists must get out of Taiwan. The Chinese people are determined to liberate Taiwan.

In commemorating the 20th anniversary of victory in the War of Resistance Against Japan, we must also point out in all solemnity that the Japanese militarists fostered by U.S. imperialism will certainly receive still severer punishment if they ignore the firm opposition of the Japanese people and the people of Asia, again indulge in their pipe-dreams and resume their old road of aggression in Asia.

U.S. imperialism is preparing a world war. But can this save it from its doom? World War I was followed by the birth of the socialist Soviet Union. World War II was followed by the emergence of a series of socialist countries and many nationally independent countries. If the U.S. imperialists should insist on launching a third world war, it can be stated categorically that many more hundreds of millions of people will turn to socialism; the imperialists will then have little room left on the globe; and it is possible that the whole structure of imperialism will collapse.

We are optimistic about the future of the world. We are confident that the people will bring to an end the epoch of wars in human history. Comrade Mao Tse-tung pointed out long ago that war, this monster, "will be finally be eliminated by the progress of human society, and in the not too distant future too. But there is only one way to eliminate it, and that is to oppose war with war, to oppose counter-revolutionary war with revolutionary war."[3]

All people's suffering from U.S. imperialist aggression, oppression and plunder, unite! Hold aloft the just banner of people's war and fight for the cause of world peace, national liberation, people's democracy and socialism! Victory will certainly go to the people of the world!

Long live the victory of people's war!

1. V.I. Lenin, "For Bread and Peace", *Collected Works*, Eng. ed., Progress Publishers, Moscow, 1964, Vol. XXVI, p. 386.

2. V.I. Lenin, "The Chief Task of Our Day", *Collected Works*, Eng. ed., Progress Publishers, Moscow, 1965, Vol. XXVII, p. 162.

3. Mao Tse-tung, "Problems of Strategy in China's Revolutionary War", *Selected Works*, Eng. ed., FLP, Peking, 1965, Vol. I, p. 182.

Speech at the Celebration Rally (1966)

Comrades and Friends,

Today is the great festival of the 17th anniversary of the founding of the People's Republic of China. On behalf of our great leader, Chairman Mao, the Central Committee of the Party and the Government of the People's Republic of China, I most warmly salute the workers, peasants and soldiers, the revolutionary teachers and students, the revolutionary Red Guards and other militant youth organizations, the revolutionary people of all nationalities and the revolutionary cadres throughout the country, and extend a hearty welcome to our friends from different countries of the world

The 17 years that have elapsed since the founding of the People's Republic of China have been no ordinary years. They are years which have witnessed earth-shaking changes in China. And they are also years which have witnessed earth-shaking changes in the world.

In the short space of 17 years, the Chinese people have completely changed the face of old China. This is a highly meritorious deed performed by the masses of the Chinese people under the leadership of Comrade Mao Zedong. We are convinced that all the oppressed peoples and nations of the world will take their own paths in the light of their own countries' conditions and seize final victory as the Chinese people did.

Today, we are celebrating this great festival amid an upsurge of the great proletarian cultural revolution. This is a great revolution, an entirely new and creative revolution carried out after the seizure of political power by the proletariat. Its aim is to overthrow through struggle the small handful of persons within the Party who are in authority who have taken the capitalist road, to sweep away all ghosts and monsters in our society., and to break the old ideas, culture, customs and habits of the exploiting classes and foster the new ideas, culture, customs and habits of the proletariat, with a view to further consolidating the dictatorship of the proletariat and developing the socialist system. The historical experience of the dictatorship of the proletariat in the world teaches us that if we fail to do this, the rule of revisionism will come about and the restoration of capitalism will take place. Should this happen in our country, China would go back to its former colonial and semi-colonial, feudal and semi-feudal road, and the imperialists and reactionaries would again ride roughshod over the people. The importance of our great cultural revolution is therefore perfectly clear.

At present, hundreds of millions of people have been aroused. The revolutionary people feel proud and elated, while the reactionary bourgeoisie has been completely discredited. We are forging ahead. We have already laid the corner-stone for a great victory.

The great proletarian cultural revolution is promoting the revolutionization of people's minds and has thus become a powerful motive force for the development of socialist production in our country. This year is the first year of our Third Five-Year Plan. The plan for this year's industrial production is expected to be over fulfilled, and agriculture promises another good harvest. New heights are being scaled in China's science and technology. Our great motherland has never been so prosperous and so full of vigour. Our national defence has never been so strong.

Chairman Mao long ago pointed out that the class struggle between the proletariat and the bourgeoisie and the struggle between the capitalist and socialist roads exists throughout the historical period of socialism. The great proletarian cultural revolution constitutes a new stage in the struggle between the two classes and between the two roads. In the course of this revolution, the struggle is still going on between the revolutionary proletarian line represented by Chairman Mao and the bourgeois line of opposing revolution. Those who cling to the erroneous line are only a small handful of persons who divorce themselves from the people, oppose the people and Mao Zedong's thought, and this spells their certain failure.

Comrades and friends! At present, an excellent situation prevails in the world. The great upheavals of the past few years in the world show that the days of imperialism headed by the United States, modern revisionism and all reaction are numbered.

U.S. imperialism is trying hard to find a way out by launching a world war. We must take this seriously. The focal point of this present struggle lies in Vietnam. We have made every preparation. Not flinching from maximum national sacrifices, we are determined to five firm support to the fraternal Vietnamese people in carrying the war of resistance against U.S. aggression and for national salvation through to the end. Imperialism headed by the United States and modern revisionism with the leadership of the CPSU as its centre are colluding and actively plotting peace talk swindles for the purpose of stamping out the raging flames of the Vietnamese people's national revolutionary war against the U.S. aggression, of the national revolutionary struggles in Asian, African and Latin American countries and of the world revolution. They will not succeed in their schemes so long as the people of the whole world keep their eyes wide open. Twenty years ago, Chairman Mao said that the people of the whole world must form a united front against U.S. imperialism so as to defeat it. The revolutionary people of all countries are now advancing along this road.

Chairman Mao has said,

People of the world, be courageous, dare to fight, defy difficulties and advance wave upon wave. Then the whole world will belong to the people. Monsters of all kinds shall be destroyed.

Such is the inevitable future of the world.

The Chinese people will continue to hold high the banner of Marxism-Leninism and the banner of proletarian internationalism and, with the Marxist-Leninists of the whole world and the revolutionary people of all countries, carry the struggle against U.S. imperialism and its lackeys and the struggle against modern revisionism with the leadership of the CPSU as its centre through to the end!

Comrades and friends!

All our achievements and successes have been scored under the wise leadership of Chairman Mao and represent the victory of Mao Zedong's thought. We must use Mao Zedong's thought to unify the thinking of the whole Party and the thinking of the people of the whole country. We must hold high the great red banner of Mao Zedong's thought and further unfold the mass movement for the creative study and application of Chairman Mao's thought throughout the country. We must turn the whole country into a great school of Mao Zedong's thought. We must build our great motherland into a still more powerful and prosperous country. This is the demand of the Chinese people as well as the hope placed in us by the people of all countries.

Long live the people of all nationalities in China!

Long live the great unity of the people of the world!

Long live the People's Republic of China!

Long live the Communist Party of China!

Long live the ever-victorious thought of Mao Zedong!

Long live our great leader Chairman Mao, and long life, long, long life to him!

Lin Biao addresses the Peking celebration rally, October 1, 1966.

Foreword to the Second Edition of Quotations of Chairman Mao Tse-tung ("The Little Red Book")

Study Chairman Mao's writings, follow his teachings and act according to his instructions

Comrade Mao Tse-tung is the greatest Marxist-Leninist of our era. He has inherited, defended and developed Marxism-Leninism with genius, creatively and comprehensively and has brought it to a higher and completely new stage.

Mao Tse-tung's thought is Marxism-Leninism of the era in which imperialism is heading for total collapse and socialism is advancing to world-wide victory. It is a powerful ideological weapon for opposing imperialism and for opposing revisionism and dogmatism. Mao Tse-tung's thought is the guiding principle for all the work of The Party, the army and the country.

Therefore, the most fundamental task in our Party's political and ideological work is at all times to hold high the great red banner of Mao Tse-tung's thought, to arm the minds of the people throughout the country with it and to persist in using it to command every field of activity. The broad masses of the workers, peasants and soldiers and the broad ranks of the revolutionary cadres and the intellectuals should really master Mao Tse-tung's thought; they should all study Chairman Mao's writings, follow his teachings, act according to his instructions and be his good fighters.

In studying the works of Chairman Mao, one should have specific problems in mind, study and apply his works in a creative way, combine study with application, first study what must be urgently applied so as to get quick results, and strive hard to apply what one is studying. In order really to master

Mao Tse-tung's thought, it is essential to study many of Chairman Mao's basic concepts over and over again, and it is best to memorize important statements and study and apply them repeatedly. The newspapers should regularly carry quotations from Chairman Mao relevant to current issues for readers to study and apply. The experience of the broad masses in their creative study and application of Chairman Mao's works in the last few years has proved that to study selected Quotations from Chairman Mao with specific problems in mind is a good way to learn Mao Tse-tung's thought, a method conducive to quick results.

We have compiled Quotations of Chairman Mao Tse-tung in order to help the broad masses learn Mao Tse-tung's thought more effectively. In organizing their study, units should select passages that is relevant to the situation, their tasks, the current thinking of their personnel, and the state of their work. In our great motherland, a new era is emerging in which the workers, peasants and soldiers are grasping Marxism-Leninism, Mao Tse-tung's thought. Once Mao Tse-tung's thought is grasped by the broad masses, it becomes a source of strength and a spiritual atom bomb of infinite power. The large-scale publication of Quotations from Chairman Mao Tse-tung is a vital measure for enabling the broad masses to grasp Mao Tse-tung's thought and for promoting the revolutionization of our people's thinking. It is our hope that all comrades will learn earnestly and diligently, bring about a new nation-wide high tide in the creative study and application of Chairman Mao's works and, under the great red banner of Mao Tse-tung's thought, strive to build our country into a great socialist state with modern agriculture, modern industry, modern science and culture and modern national defence!

Speech at the Peking Rally Commemorating the 50th Anniversary of the October Revolution

Comrades, Young Red Guard Fighters and Friends:

Today the Chinese people join the proletarians and revolutionary people throughout the world in grand and solemn commemoration of the 50th anniversary of the Great October Socialist Revolution.

The October Revolution led by the great Lenin was a turning point in human history.

The victory of the October Revolution broke through the dark rule of capitalism, established the first state of the dictatorship of the proletariat in the world and opened a new era of the world proletarian revolution.

For more than one hundred years since Marx and Engels formulated the theory of scientific socialism, the international proletariat, advancing wave upon wave and making heroic sacrifices, has been waging arduous struggles for the great ideal of communism and has performed immortal exploits in the cause of the emancipation of mankind.

In his struggle against the revisionism of the Second International and the great practice of leading the October Socialist Revolution, Lenin solved a series of problems of the proletarian revolution and the dictatorship of the proletariat as well as the problem of victory for socialism in one country, thus developing Marxism to the stage of Leninism. Leninism is Marxism in the era of imperialism and proletarian revolution. The salvoes of the October Revolution brought Leninism to all countries so that the world took on an entirely new look.

In the last fifty years following the road of the October

Revolution under the banner of Marxism-Leninism, the proletariat and the revolutionary people of the world have carried the world history forward to an entirely new the era in which imperialism is heading for collapse and socialism is advancing to worldwide victory. It is a great new era in which the proletariat and the bourgeoisie are locked in the decisive battle on a world wide scale.

Led by the great leader Chairman Mao, the Chinese people have followed up their victory in the national-democratic revolution with greatest victories in the socialist revolution and socialist construction. Socialist China has become the mighty bulwark of world revolution. Adhering to the road of the October Revolution, the heroic people of Albania have raised a bright red banner in Europe. By their war against U.S. imperialist aggression and for national salvation, the Vietnamese people have set a brilliant example of struggle against imperialism for the people of the whole world. The movement of national-democratic liberation in Asia, Africa and Latin America is developing vigorously. The ranks of the Marxist-Leninists are growing steadily, and a new situation has emerged in the international communist movement.

Compared with half a century ago, the world proletarian revolution today is deeper in content and far broader in scope and far sharper in its struggle. The new historical era has posed a series of important new problems for Marxist-Leninists. However, in the final analysis, the most fundamental problem remains that of seizing and consolidating political power.

Chairman Mao says: **"The aim of every revolutionary struggle in the world is the seizure and consolidation of political power."** This is the great Marxist-Leninist truth.

The struggle between the Marxist-Leninist and the revisionists always focuses on this fundamental issue. The modern revisionists, represented by Khrushchev and his successors, Brezhnev and Kosygin and company, are wildly opposing the revolution of the people of the world and have

76

openly abandoned the dictatorship of the proletariat and brought about and all-round capitalist restoration in the Soviet Union. This is a monstrous betrayal of the October Revolution. This is a monstrous betrayal of Marxism-Leninism. It is a monstrous betrayal of the great Soviet people and the people of the whole world. Therefore, if the proletariat fails to smash the wanton attacks of the modern revisionists, if it does not firmly defend the road of the October Revolution opened up by the great Lenin, continue to advance along this road under the new historical conditions and thoroughly solve the question of how to seize and consolidate political power, it will not be able to win the final victory, or will probably loose political power even after seizing it, and, like the Soviet people, will come under the rule of a new privileged bourgeois stratum.

It is our good fortune that because Comrade Mao Tse-tung has comprehensively inherited and developed the teachings of Marx, Engels, Lenin and Stalin on proletarian revolution and the dictatorship of the proletariat, the must fundamental issue of the world proletarian revolution, that is, the road to the seizure of the consolidation of political power, has been brought to a higher stage in theory and in practice. Our great leader Chairman Mao has developed Marxism-Leninism and raised it to an entirely new peak. The ever-victorious thought of Mao Tse-tung is Marxism-Leninism in the era in which imperialism is heading for total collapse and socialism is advancing toward worldwide victory.

In the course of leading the great struggle of the Chinese revolution, Chairman Mao has with genius solved a whole series of complicated problems concerning the seizure of power by force of arms. Under his leadership, the Chinese people went through the most protracted, fierce, arduous and complex people's revolutionary war in the history of the world proletarian revolution and founded the red political power, the dictatorship of the proletariat.

The way the Chinese people seized political power by

force of arms under Chairman Mao's leadership may be summarized as follows: Under the leadership of the political party of the proletariat, to arouse the peasant masses in the countryside to wage guerrilla war, unfold an agrarian revolution, build rural base areas, use the countryside to encircle the cities and finally capture the cities. This is a great new development of the road of to the seizure of political power by force or arms indicated by the October Revolution.

Chairman Mao has said: **"As a rule, revolution starts, grows and triumphs first in those places in which the counter-revolutionary forces are comparatively weak.".** Since in our time all the reactionary ruling classes have a tight grip on the main cities, it is necessary for a revolutionary political party to utilize the vulnerable links and areas of reactionary rule, fully arouse the masses, conduct guerrilla warfare, establish stable revolutionary bases and so build up and temper their own forces and, through prolonged fighting, strive step by step for complete victory in the revolution. Hence, reliance on the masses to build revolutionary base areas and use the countryside to encircle the cities is a historic task which the oppressed nations and peoples in the world today must seriously study and tackle in their fight to seize political power by force of arms.

Not only has Comrade Mao Tse-tung creatively developed Leninism on the question of the seizure of political power by the proletariat, he has made an epoch-making creative development of Leninism on the most important question of our time - the question of consolidating the dictatorship of the proletariat and preventing the restoration of capitalism.

From the first day of the victory of the October Revolution, Lenin paid close attention to the consolidation of the new-born Soviet state power. He recognized the sharp and protracted nature of class struggle under the dictatorship of the proletariat, pointing out that **"the transition from capitalism to communism takes an entire historical epoch. Until this**

epoch is over, the exploiters inevitably cherish the hope of restoration, and this hope turns into attempts at restoration."

The biggest lesson in the history of the international communist movement in the last fifty years is the restoration of capitalism in the Soviet Union and other socialist countries. This harsh fact has strikingly brought the Marxist-Leninists of the world face to face with the question of how to consolidate the dictatorship of the proletariat and prevent the restoration of capitalism.

It is Comrade Mao Tse-tung, the great leader of the world proletariat of our time, who in the new historical conditions, has systematically summed up the historical experience of the dictatorship of the proletariat in the world, scientifically analysed the contradictions in socialist society, profoundly shown the laws of class struggle in socialist society and put forward a whole set of theory, line, principles, methods and policies for the continuation of revolution under the dictatorship of the proletariat. With supreme courage and wisdom, Chairman Mao has successfully led the first great proletarian cultural revolution in history. This is an extremely important landmark, demonstrating that Marxism-Leninism has developed into the stage of Mao Tse-tung's thought.

The victory of the great proletarian revolution has opened up in China, which has a quarter of the world's population, a bright path for consolidating the dictatorship of the proletariat and for carrying the socialist revolution through to the end. The proletariat and the revolutionary people of the world who are fighting imperialism, modern revisionism and all reaction resolutely support our great proletarian cultural revolution. They find in the victory of this revolution tremendous inspiration, bright prospects and greater confidence in victory.

The imperialists headed by the United States and their lackeys the modern revisionists and all the reactionaries have taken great pains to curse and vilify our great proletarian cultural revolution. This proves by negative example that our victory has dealt the enemy a very heavy blow and that they are nothing but a bunch of vampires that are bound to be destroyed.

The world is moving forward. And theory which reflects the laws of the world, is likewise developing continuously.

Mao Tse-tung's thought is the banner of our era.

Once Mao Tse-tung's thought - Marxist-Leninist at its highest in the present era - is grasped, the oppressed nations and peoples will, through their own struggles, be able to win liberation.

Once Mao Tse-tung's thought - Marxism-Leninism at its highest in the present era - is grasped, the people of those countries where political power has been usurped by the revisionists will, through their own struggles, be able to overthrow the rule of revisionism and re-establish the dictatorship of the proletariat.

Once Marxism-Leninism, Mao Tse-tung's thought is integrated with the revolutionary practice of the people of all countries, the entire old world will be shattered to smithereens.

Comrades, young Red Guard fighters and friends:

The fifty years since the October Revolution have been years of fierce struggle between socialism and capitalism and between Marxism-Leninism and modern revisionism., with the former winning one victory after an other. The imperialist system resembles a dying person who is sinking fast, like the sun setting beyond the western hills. The emergence of Khrushchov revisionism is a product of imperialist policy and reflects the death-bed struggle of imperialism. Although imperialism and revisionism will go on making trouble in collusion with each other, the reactionary adverse current can, after all, never become the main current. The dialectics of history is irresistible. Henceforth the proletariat and the revolutionary people of the world will raise still higher the great red banner of Marxism-Leninism, Mao Tse-tung's thought, and march forward in giant strides along the road opened up by the October Revolution!

Those who betray the October Revolution can never escape the punishment of history. Khrushchov has long since fallen. In redoubling its efforts to peruse the policy of betrayal, the Brezhnev-Kosygin clique will not last long either. The proletariat and the working people of the Soviet Union, with their glorious tradition of revolution, will never forget the teachings of the great Lenin and Stalin. They are sure to rise in revolution under the banner of Leninism, overthrow the rule of the reactionary revisionist clique and bring the Soviet Union back into the orbit of socialism.

Comrades, young Red Guard fighters and friends!

The situation in our great motherland is excellent. Under the guidance of the latest instructions of the great leader Chairman Mao, the great proletarian cultural revolution is forging ahead victoriously.

We must raise still higher the great banner of the October Revolution and the great banner of Marxism-Leninism, Mao Tse-tung's thought, and carry the great proletarian cultural revolution through to the end.

We must build our great motherland into a still more powerful base for world revolution.

We must give ever more vigorous support to the revolutionary struggles of the proletariat and the people of all countries.

We must together with the revolutionary people everywhere, carry through to the end the struggle against U.S.-led imperialism and against modern revisionism with the Soviet revisionist renegade clique at its centre.

We must intensify our efforts in studying and mastering Mao Tse-tung's thought and disseminate it still more widely throughout the world.

These are glorious tasks entrusted to the people of our country by history, and they are our incumbent internationalist duty.

Our great leader Chairman Mao has given the call: **"Let the Marxist-Leninists of all countries unite, let the revolutionary people of the whole world unite and overthrow imperialism, modern revisionism and all reaction. A new world without imperialism, without capitalism and without exploitation of man by may will surely be built."**

Let us fight with courage for the realization of this great call of Chairman Mao's!

Long live the Great October Socialist Revolution!

Long live the great proletarian cultural revolution!

Workers of all countries unite!

Workers of all countries unite with the oppressed peoples and oppressed nations!

Long live the invincible Marxism, Leninism, Mao Tse-tung's thought!

Long live the great teacher, great leader, great supreme commander, great helmsman Chairman Mao! A long, long life to him!

Report to the Ninth National Congress of the Communist Party of China

(Delivered on April 1 and adopted on April 14, 1969)

Comrades!

The Ninth National Congress of the Communist Party of China will be a congress with a far-reaching influence in the history of our Party.

Our present congress is convened at a time when great victory has been won in the Great Proletarian Cultural Revolution personally initiated and led by Chairman Mao. This great revolutionary storm has shattered the bourgeois headquarters headed December by the renegade, hidden traitor and scab Liu Shao-chi, exposed the handful of renegades, enemy agents and absolutely unrepentant persons in power taking the capitalist road within the Party, with Liu Shao-chi as their arch-representative, and smashed their plot to restore capitalism; it has tremendously strengthened the dictatorship of the proletariat in our country, tremendously strengthened our Party and thus prepared ample conditions for this congress politically, ideologically and organizationally.

I. ON THE PREPARATION FOR THE GREAT PROLETARIAN CULTURAL REVOLUTION

China's Great Proletarian Cultural Revolution is a genuine proletarian revolution on an immense scale.

Chairman Mao has explained the necessity of the current great revolution in concise terms:

The current Great Proletarian Cultural Revolution is absolutely necessary and most timely for consolidating the

dictatorship of the proletariat, preventing capitalist restoration and building socialism.

In order to comprehend this scientific thesis of Chairman Mao's fully, we should have a deep understanding of his theory of continuing the revolution under the dictatorship of the proletariat.

In 1957, shortly after the conclusion of the Party's Eighth National Congress, Chairman Mao made public his great work *On the Correct Handling of Contradictions Among the People*, in which, following his *Report to the Second Plenary Session of the Seventh Central Committee of the Communist Party of China*, he comprehensively set forth the existence of contradictions, classes and class struggle under the conditions of the dictatorship of the proletariat, set forth the thesis of the existence of two different types of contradictions in socialist society, those between ourselves and the enemy and those among the people, and set forth the great theory of continuing the revolution under the dictatorship of the proletariat. This great work, like a radiant beacon, illuminates the course of China's socialist revolution and socialist construction and it has laid the theoretical foundation for the current Great Proletarian Cultural Revolution.

In order to have a deeper understanding of Chairman Mao's great historic contribution, it is necessary briefly to review the historical experience of the international communist movement.

In 1852, Marx said:

Long before me bourgeois historians had described the historical development of this class struggle and bourgeois economists the economic anatomy of the classes. What I did that was new was to prove: 1) that the *existence of classes* **is only bound up with** *particular historical phases in the development of production,* 2) **that the class struggle necessarily leads to the** *dictatorship of the proletariat, 3)* **that**

this dictatorship itself only constitutes the transition to the *abolition of all classes* **and to a** *classless society.* (Marx and Engels, *Selected Correspondence*, Chinese ed., p. 63.)

Marx's theory of the dictatorship of the proletariat clearly distinguished scientific socialism from utopian socialism and sham socialism of every kind. Marx and Engels fought all their lives for this theory and for its realization.

After the death of Marx and Engels, almost all the parties of the Second International betrayed Marxism, with the exception of the Bolshevik Party led by Lenin. Lenin inherited, defended and developed Marxism in the struggle against the revisionism of the Second International. The struggle focused on the question of the dictatorship of the proletariat. In denouncing the old revisionists, Lenin time and again stated:

Those who recognize *only* **the class struggle are not yet Marxists.... Only he is a Marxist who extends the recognition of the class struggle to the recognition of the** *dictatorship of the proletariat.* (Lenin, *Collected Works*, Chinese ed., Vol. 25, p. 399.)

Lenin led the proletariat of Russia in winning the victory of the Great October Socialist Revolution and founding the first socialist state. Through his great revolutionary practice in leading the dictatorship of the proletariat, Lenin perceived the danger of the restoration of capitalism and the protracted nature of class struggle:

The transition from capitalism to Communism represents an entire historical epoch. Until this epoch has terminated, the exploiters inevitably cherish the hope of restoration, and this hope is converted into *attempts* **at restoration**. (Lenin, *Collected Works*, Chinese ed., Vol. 28, p. 235.)

Lenin stated: **...the bourgeoisie, whose resistance is increased** *tenfold* **by its overthrow (even if only in one country), and whose power lies not only in the strength of** international capital, in the strength and durability of the international connections of the bourgeoisie, but also in the *force of habit,* in the strength of *small production.* **For, unfortunately, small production is still very, very widespread in the world, and small production** *engenders* **capitalism and the bourgeoisie continuously, daily, hourly, spontaneously, and on a mass scale**. (Lenin, *Collected Works,* Chinese ed., Vol. 31, p. 6.)

His conclusion was: **"For all these reasons the dictatorship of the proletariat is essential.";** *(Ibid.)*

Lenin also stated that **"the new bourgeoisie"** was **"arising from among our Soviet government employees".** (Lenin, *Collected Works,* Chinese ed., Vol. 29, p. 162.)

He pointed out that the danger of restoration also came from capitalist encirclement: The imperialist countries **"will never miss an opportunity for military intervention, as they put it, i.e., to strangle Soviet power".** (Lenin, *Collected Works,* Chinese ed. Vol. 31, p. 423.)

The Soviet revisionist renegade clique has completely betrayed these brilliant teachings of Lenin's. From Khrushchov to Brezhnev and company, they are all persons in power taking the capitalist road, who had long concealed themselves in the Communist Party of the Soviet Union. As soon as they came to power, they turned the bourgeoisie's **"hope of restoration"** into *"attempts* **at restoration",** usurped the leadership of the Party of Lenin and Stalin and, through "peaceful evolution", turned the world's first state under the dictatorship of the proletariat into a dark fascist state under the dictatorship of the bourgeoisie.

Chairman Mao has waged a tit-for-tat struggle against modern revisionism with the Soviet revisionist renegade clique as its centre and has inherited, defended and developed the Marxist-Leninist theory of proletarian revolution and the dictatorship of the proletariat. Chairman Mao has comprehensively summed up the historical experience both positive and negative, of the dictatorship of the proletariat and, in order to prevent the restoration of capitalism, has put forward the theory of continuing the revolution under the dictatorship of the proletariat.

As early as March 1949, on the eve of the transition of the Chinese revolution from the new-democratic revolution to the socialist revolution, Chairman Mao explicitly pointed out in his report to the Second Plenary Session of the Seventh Central Committee of the Party: After the country-wide seizure of power by the proletariat, the principal internal contradiction is **"the contradiction between the working class and the bourgeoisie"**. The heart of the struggle is still the question of state power. Chairman Mao especially reminded us:

After the enemies with guns have been wiped out, there will still be enemies without guns; they are bound to struggle desperately against us, and we must never regard these enemies lightly. If we do not now raise and understand the problem in this way, we shall commit the gravest mistakes.

Having foreseen the protracted and complex nature of the class struggle between the proletariat and the bourgeoisie after the establishment of the dictatorship of the proletariat, Chairman Mao set the whole Party the militant task of fighting imperialism, the Kuomintang and the bourgeoisie in the political, ideological, economic, cultural and diplomatic spheres.

Our Party waged intense battles in accordance with the resolution of the Second Plenary Session of the Seventh Central Committee and the Party's general line for the transition period formulated by Chairman Mao. By 1956, the socialist transformation of the ownership of the means of production in agriculture, handicrafts and capitalist industry and commerce had been in the main completed. That was the crucial moment for deciding whether the socialist revolution could continue to advance. In view of the rampancy of revisionism in the international communist movement and the new trends of class struggle in our country, Chairman Mao, in his great work *On the Correct Handling of Contradictions Among the People,* called the attention of the whole Party to the following fact:

In China, although in the main socialist transformation has been completed with respect to the system of ownership...there are still remnants of the overthrown landlord and comprador classes, there is still a bourgeoisie, and the remoulding of the petty bourgeoisie has only just started.

Countering the fallacy put forward by Liu Shao-chi in 1956 that **"in China, the question of which wins out, socialism or capitalism, is already solved"** Chairman Mao specifically pointed out: **"The question of which will win out, socialism or capitalism, is still not really settled." "The class struggle between the proletariat and the bourgeoisie, the class struggle between the different political forces, and the class struggle in the ideological field between the proletariat and the bourgeoisie will continue to be long and tortuous and at times will even become very acute."** Thus, for the first time in the theory and practice of the international communist movement, it was pointed out explicitly that classes and class struggle still exist after the socialist transformation of the ownership of the means of production has been in the main completed, and that the proletariat must continue the revolution.

The proletarian headquarters headed by Chairman Mao led the broad masses in carrying on the great struggle in the direction he indicated. From the struggle against the bourgeois rightists in 1957 to the struggle to uncover Peng Teh-huai's anti-Party clique at the Lushan Meeting in 1959, from the great debate on the general line of the Party in building socialism to the struggle between the two lines in the socialist education movement--the focus of the struggle was the question of whether to take the socialist road or to take the capitalist road, whether to uphold the dictatorship of the proletariat or to restore the dictatorship of the. bourgeoisie.

Every single victory of Chairman Mao's proletarian revolutionary line, every victory in every major campaign launched by the Party against the bourgeoisie, was gained only after smashing the revisionist line represented by Liu Shao-chi, which either was Right or was "Left" in form but Right in essence.

Now it has been proved through investigation that Liu Shao-chi betrayed the Party, capitulated to the enemy and became a hidden traitor and scab as far back as the First Revolutionary Civil War period, that he was a crime-steeped lackey of the imperialists, modern revisionists and Kuomintang reactionaries and that he was the arch-representative of the persons in power taking the capitalist road. He had a political line by which he vainly attempted to restore capitalism in China and turn her into an imperialist and revisionist colony. In addition, he had an organizational line to serve his counter-revolutionary political line. For many years, recruiting deserters and turncoats, Liu Shao-chi gathered together a gang of renegades, enemy agents and capitalist-roaders in power. They covered up their counter-revolutionary political records, shielded each other, colluded in doing evil, usurped important Party and government posts and controlled the leadership in many central and local units, thus forming an underground bourgeois headquarters in opposition to the proletarian headquarters headed by Chairman Mao. They collaborated with the imperialists, modern revisionists and Kuomintang reactionaries and played the kind of disruptive role that the U.S. imperialists, the Soviet revisionists and the reactionaries of various countries were unable to do.

In 1939, when the War of Resistance Against Japan and for National Liberation led by Chairman Mao was vigorously surging forward, Liu Shao-chi came up with his sinister book *Self-Cultivation.* The core of that book was the betrayal of the dictatorship of the proletariat. It did not touch at all upon the questions of defeating Japanese imperialism and of waging the struggle against the Kuomintang reactionaries, nor did it touch upon the fundamental Marxist-Leninist principle of seizing state power by armed force; on the contrary, it urged Communist Party members to depart from the great practice of revolution and indulge in idealistic "self-cultivation", which actually meant that Communists should "cultivate" themselves into willing slaves going down on their knees before the counter-revolutionary dictatorship of the imperialists and the Kuomintang reactionaries.

After the victory of the War of Resistance Against Japan, when the U.S. imperialists were arming Chiang Kai-shek's counter-revolutionary troops in preparation for launching an all-out offensive against the liberated areas, Liu Shao-chi, catering to the needs of the U.S.-Chiang reactionaries, dished up the capitulationist line, alleging that "China has entered the new stage of peace and democracy". It was designed to oppose Chairman Mao's general line of **"go all out to mobilize the masses, expand the people's forces and, under the leadership of our Party, defeat the aggressor and build a new China"**, and to oppose Chairman Mao's policy of **"give tit for tat and fight for every inch of land"**, which was adopted to counter the offensive of the U.S.-Chiang reactionaries. Liu Shao-chi preached that "at present the main form of the struggle of the Chinese revolution has changed from armed struggle to non-armed and mass parliamentary struggle". He tried to abolish the Party's leadership over the people's armed forces and to "unify" the Eighth Route Army and the New Fourth Army, predecessors of the People's Liberation Army, into Chiang Kai-shek's "national army" and to demobilize large numbers of worker and peasant soldiers led by the Party in a vain attempt to eradicate the people's armed forces, strangle the Chinese revolution and obeisantly hand over to the Kuomintang the fruits of victory which the Chinese people had won in blood.

In April 1949, on the eve of the countrywide victory of

China's new-democratic revolution when the Chinese People's Liberation Army was preparing to cross the Yangtse River, Liu Shao-chi hurried to Tientsin and threw himself into the arms of the capitalists. He fiercely opposed the policy of utilizing, restricting and transforming private capitalist industry, a policy decided upon by the Second Plenary Session of the Seventh Central Committee of the Party which had just concluded. He clamoured that "capitalism in China today is still in its youth", that it needed an unlimited "big expansion" and that "capitalist exploitation today is no crime, it is a merit". He shamelessly praised the capitalist class, saying that "the more they exploit, the greater their merit", and feverishly advertised the revisionist theory of productive forces. He did all this in his futile attempt to lead China onto the capitalist road.

In short, at the many important historical junctures of the new-democratic revolution and the socialist revolution, Liu Shao-chi and his gang always wantonly opposed Chairman Mao's proletarian revolutionary line and engaged in counter-revolutionary conspiratorial and disruptive activities. However, since they were counter-revolutionaries, their plots were bound to come to light eventually. When Khrushchov came to power, and especially when the Soviet revisionists ganged up with the U.S. imperialists and the reactionaries of India and other countries in whipping up a large-scale anti-China campaign, Liu Shao-chi and his gang became all the more rabid.

Chairman Mao was the first to perceive the danger of the counter-revolutionary plots of Liu Shao-chi and his gang. At the working conference of the Central Committee in January 1962, Chairman Mao pointed out the necessity of guarding against the emergence of revisionism. At the working conference of the Central Committee at Peitaiho in August 1962 and at the Tenth Plenary Session of the Eighth Central Committee of the Party in September of the same year, Chairman Mao put forward more comprehensively the basic line of our Party for the whole historical period of socialism. Chairman Mao pointed out:

Socialist society covers a considerably long historical period. In the historical period of socialism, there are still classes, class contradictions and class struggle, there is the struggle between the socialist road and the capitalist road, and there is the danger of capitalist restoration. We must recognize the protracted and complex nature of this struggle. We must heighten our vigilance. We must conduct socialist education. We must correctly understand and handle class contradictions and class struggle, distinguish the contradictions between ourselves and the enemy from those among the people and handle them correctly. Otherwise a socialist country like ours will turn into its opposite and degenerate, and a capitalist restoration will take place. From now on we must remind ourselves of this every year, every month and every day so that we can retain a rather sober understanding of this problem and have a Marxist-Leninist line.

This Marxist-Leninist line advanced by Chairman Mao is the lifeline of our Party. Following this, in May 1963, under the direction of Chairman Mao, the *Draft Decision of the Central Committee of the Chinese Communist Party on Certain Problems in Our Present Rural Work (i.e., the 10-Point Decision)* was worked out, which laid down the line, principles and policies of the Party for the socialist education movement. Chairman Mao again warned the whole Party: If classes and class struggle were forgotten and if the dictatorship of the proletariat were forgotten, **"then it would not be long, perhaps only several years or a decade, or several decades at most, before a counter-revolutionary restoration on a national scale would inevitably occur, the Marxist-Leninist party would undoubtedly become a revisionist party, a fascist party, and the whole of China would change its colour. Comrades, please think it over. What a dangerous situation this would be!"** Thus Chairman Mao still more sharply showed the whole Party and the people of the whole country the danger of the restoration of capitalism.

All these warnings and struggles did not and could not in the least change the reactionary class nature of Liu Shao-chi and his gang. In 1964, in the great socialist education movement, Liu Shao-chi came out and repressed the masses, shielded the capitalist-roaders in power and openly attacked the Marxist scientific method of investigating and studying social conditions initiated by Chairman Mao, branding it as "outdated". He raved that whoever refused to carry out his line was "not qualified to hold a leading post". He and his gang were working against time to restore capitalism. At the end of 1964, Chairman Mao convened a working conference of the Central Committee and, under his direction, the document *Some Current Problems Raised in the Socialist Education Movement in the Rural Areas (i.e., the 23-Point Document)* was drawn up. He denounced Liu Shao-chi's bourgeois reactionary line which was "Left" in form but Right in essence and repudiated Liu Shao-chi's absurdities, such as "the intertwining of the contradictions inside and outside the Party" and "the contradiction between the 'four cleans'" and the 'four uncleans'". And for the first time Chairman Mao specifically indicated: **"The main target of the present movement is those Party persons in power taking the capitalist road."** This new conclusion drawn by Chairman Mao after summing up the historical experience of the dictatorship of the proletariat, domestic and international, set right the course of the socialist education movement and clearly showed the orientation for the approaching Great Proletarian Cultural Revolution.

Reviewing the history of this period, we can see that the current Great Proletarian Cultural Revolution with the participation of hundreds of millions of revolutionary people has occurred by no means accidentally. It is the inevitable result of the protracted and sharp struggle between the two classes, the two roads and the two lines in socialist society. The Great Proletarian Cultural Revolution is **"a great political revolution carried out by the proletariat against the bourgeoisie and all other exploiting classes; it is a continuation of the prolonged**

93

struggle waged by the Chinese Communist Party and the masses of revolutionary people under its leadership against the Kuomintang reactionaries, a continuation of the class struggle between the proletariat and the bourgeoisie." The heroic Chinese proletariat, poor and lower-middle peasants, People's Liberation Army, revolutionary cadres and revolutionary intellectuals, who were all determined to follow the great leader Chairman Mao closely in taking the socialist road, could no longer tolerate the restoration activities of Liu Shao-chi and his gang, and so a great class battle was unavoidable.

As Chairman Mao pointed out in his talk in February 1967:

In the past we waged struggles in rural areas, in factories, in the cultural field, and we carried out the socialist education movement. But all this failed to solve the problem because we did not find a form, a method, to arouse the broad masses to expose our dark aspect openly, in an all-round way and from below.

Now we have found this form--it is the Great Proletarian Cultural Revolution. It is only by arousing the masses in their hundreds of millions to air their viewsfreely, write big-character posters and hold great debates that the renegades, enemy agents and capitalist-roaders in power who have wormed their way into the Party can be exposed and their plots to restore capitalism smashed. It was precisely with the participation of the broad masses in the examination of Liu Shao-chi's case that his true features as an old-line counter-revolutionary, renegade, hidden traitor and scab were brought to light. The Enlarged Twelfth Plenary Session of the Eighth Central Committee of the Party decided to dismiss Liu Shao-chi from all posts both inside and outside the Party and to expel him from the Party once and for all. This was a great victory for the hundreds of millions of the people. On the basis of the theory of continuing the revolution under the dictatorship of the proletariat, our great teacher

94

Chairman Mao has personally initiated and led the Great Proletarian Cultural Revolution. This is indeed **"absolutely necessary and most timely"** and it is a new and great contribution to the theory and practice of Marxism-Leninism.

II. ON THE COURSE OF THE GREAT PROLETARIAN CULTURAL REVOLUTION

The Great Proletarian Cultural Revolution is a great political revolution personally initiated and led by our great leader Chairman Mao under the conditions of the dictatorship of the proletariat, a great revolution in the realm of the superstructure. Our aim is to smash revisionism, seize back that portion of power usurped by the bourgeoisie, exercise all-round dictatorship of the proletariat in the superstructure, including all spheres of culture, and strengthen and consolidate the economic base of socialism so as to ensure that our country continues to advance in giant strides along the road of socialism.

Back in 1962, at the Tenth Plenary Session of the Eighth Central Committee of the Party, Chairman Mao pointed out:

To overthrow a political power, it is always necessary first of all to create public opinion, to do work in the ideological sphere. This is true for the revolutionary class as well as for the counter-revolutionary class.

This statement of Chairman Mao's dealt the Liu Shao-chi counter-revolutionary revisionist clique a blow at the heart. It was for the sole purpose of creating public opinion to prepare for the overthrow of the dictatorship of the proletariat that they spared no effort in seizing upon the field of ideology and the superstructure, violently exercising counter-revolutionary dictatorship over the proletariat in the various departments they controlled and wildly spreading poisonous weeds. To overthrow them politically, we must likewise first vanquish their counter-revolutionary public opinion by revolutionary public opinion.

Chairman Mao has always attached major importance to

the struggle in ideology. After the liberation of our country, he initiated many criticisms including those of the film *The Life of Wu Hsun,* the Hu Feng counter-revolutionary clique and *Studies of "The Dream of the Red Chamber"*". And this time it was Chairman Mao again who led the whole Party in launching the offensive on the positions occupied by Liu Shao-chi and his gang for the bourgeoisie. Chairman Mao wrote the celebrated essay *Where Do Correct Ideas Come from?* and other documents, in which he criticized Liu Shao-chi's bourgeois idealism and metaphysics, criticized the departments of literature and art under Liu Shao-chi's control as being **"still dominated by 'the dead'"**, criticized the Ministry of Culture by saying that **"if it refuses to change, it should be renamed the Ministry of Emperors, Kings, Generals and Ministers, the Ministry of Talents and Beauties or the Ministry of Foreign Mummies"** and said that the Ministry of Health should likewise be renamed the **"Ministry of Health for Urban Overlords"**. At the call of Chairman Mao, the proletariat first launched a revolution in the fields of Peking Opera, the ballet and symphonic music, fields that had been regarded as sacred and inviolable by the landlord and capitalist classes. It was a fight at close quarters. Despite every possible kind of resistance and sabotage by Liu Shao-chi and his gang, the proletariat finally scored important successes after arduous struggles. A number of splendid model revolutionary theatrical works appeared and the heroic figures of workers, peasants and soldiers finally took the centre of the stage. After that, Chairman Mao initiated the criticism of *Hai Jui Dismissed from Office* and other poisonous weeds, focusing the attack right on the den of the revisionist clique--that impenetrable and watertight "independent kingdom" under Liu Shao-chi's control, the old Peking Municipal Party Committee.

The *Circular* of May 16, 1966 worked out under Chairman Mao's personal guidance laid down the theory, line, principles and policies for the Great Proletarian Cultural Revolution and constituted the great programme for the whole

96

movement. The *Circular* thoroughly criticized the "February Outline" turned out by Liu Shao-chi's bourgeois headquarters for the purpose of suppressing this great revolution. It called upon the whole Party and the people of the whole country to direct the spearhead of struggle against the representatives of the bourgeoisie who had sneaked into the Party and to pay special attention to unmasking **"persons like Khrushchev...who are still nestling beside us".**" This was a great call mobilizing the people of the whole country to unfold a great political revolution. The Cultural Revolution Group Under the Central Committee, which was set up by decision of the *Circular*, has firmly carried out Chairman Mao's proletarian revolutionary line.

Under the guidance of Chairman Mao's proletarian revolutionary line, the broad revolutionary masses plunged into the fight. In Peking University a big-character poster was written in response to the call of the Central Committee. And soon big-character posters criticizing reactionary bourgeois ideas mushroomed all over the country. Then Red Guards rose and came forward in large numbers and revolutionary young people became courageous and daring pathbreakers. Thrown into a panic, the Liu Shao-chi clique rushed out with the bourgeois reactionary line, cruelly suppressing the revolutionary movement of the student youth. However, this did not win them much time in their deathbed struggle. Chairman Mao called and presided over the Eleventh Plenary Session of the Eighth Central Committee of the Party. The Plenary Session adopted the programmatic document, *Decision of the Central Committee of the Chinese Communist Party Concerning the Great Proletarian Cultural Revolution (i.e., the 16-Point Decision)*. Chairman Mao put up his big-character poster *Bombard the Headquarters*, thus taking the lid off Liu Shao-chi's bourgeois headquarters. In his letter to the Red Guards, Chairman Mao said that the revolutionary actions of the Red Guards **"express your wrath against and your denunciation of the landlord class, the bourgeoisie, the imperialists, the** revisionists and their running dogs, all of whom exploit and oppress the workers, peasants, revolutionary intellectuals and revolutionary parties and groups. They show that it is right to rebel against reactionaries. I warmly support you." Afterwards, Chairman Mao received 13 million Red Guards and other revolutionary masses from all parts of the country on eight occasions at Tien An Men in the capital, which heightened the revolutionary fighting will of the people of the whole country. The revolutionary movements of the workers, peasants and revolutionary functionaries developed rapidly. Increasing numbers of big-character posters spread like a raging prairie fire and roared like guns; the slogan **"It is right to rebel against reactionaries"** resounded throughout the land. And the battle of the people in their hundreds of millions to bombard Liu Shao-chi's bourgeois headquarters developed vigorously.

No reactionary class will ever step down from the stage of history of its own accord. When the revolution touched that portion of power usurped by the bourgeoisie, the class struggle became all the more acute. After Liu Shao-chi's downfall, his revisionist clique and his agents in various places changed their tactics time and again, putting forward slogans which were "Left" in form but Right in essence such as "suspecting all" and "overthrowing all", in a futile attempt to go on hitting hard at the many and protecting their own handful. Moreover, they created splits among the revolutionary masses and manipulated and hoodwinked a section of the masses so as to protect themselves. When these schemes were shattered by the proletarian revolutionaries, they launched another frenzied counter-attack, that is, the adverse current lasting from the winter of 1966 to the spring of 1967.

This adverse current was directed against the proletarian headquarters headed by Chairman Mao. Its general programme boiled down to this: to overthrow the decisions adopted by the Eleventh Plenary Session of the Eighth Central Committee of the Party, reversing the verdict on the overthrown bourgeois headquarters headed by Liu Shao-chi, reversing the verdict on the bourgeois reactionary line, which had already been thoroughly repudiated and discredited by the broad masses, and repressing and retaliating on the revolutionary mass movement. However, this adverse current was seriously criticized by Chairman Mao and resisted by the broad revolutionary masses; it could not prevent the main current of the revolutionary mass movement from surging forward.

The twists and reversals in the revolutionary movement further brought home to the broad masses the importance of political power: The main reason why Liu Shao-chi and his gang could do evil was that they had usurped the power of the proletariat in many units and localities, and the main reason why the revolutionary masses were repressed was that power was not in the hands of the proletariat in those places. In some units, the socialist system of ownership existed only in form, but in reality the leadership had been usurped by a handful of renegades, enemy agents and capitalist-roaders in power, or it remained in the hands of former capitalists. Especially when the capitalist-roaders in power failed in their scheme to suppress the revolution on the pretext of "grasping production" and whipped up the evil counter-revolutionary wind of economism, the broad masses came to understand still better that only by recapturing the lost power was it possible for them to defeat the capitalist-roaders in power completely. Under the leadership and with the support of Chairman Mao and the proletarian headquarters headed by him, the working class in Shanghai with its revolutionary tradition came forward courageously and, uniting with the broad revolutionary masses and revolutionary cadres, seized power from below in January 1967 from the capitalist-roaders in power in the former Municipal Party Committee and Municipal People's Council.

Chairman Mao summed up in good time the experience of the January storm of revolution in Shanghai and issued his call to the whole country: **"Proletarian revolutionaries, unite and seize power from the handful of Party persons in power taking the capitalist road!"** Following that, Chairman Mao gave the instruction: **"The People's Liberation Army should support the broad masses of the Left."** He went on to sum up the experience of Heilungkiang Province and other provinces and municipalities, laid down the principles and policies for the establishment of revolutionary committees which embrace representatives of the revolutionary cadres, representatives of the People's Liberation Army and representatives of the revolutionary masses, constituting a revolutionary three-in-one combination, and thus pushed forward the nation-wide struggle for the seizure of power.

The struggle between the proletariat and the bourgeoisie for the seizure and counter-seizure of power was a life-and-death struggle. During the year and nine months from Shanghai's January storm of revolution in 1967 to the establishment of the revolutionary committees of Tibet and Sinkiang in September 1968, repeated trials of political strength took place between the two classes and the two lines, fierce struggles went on between proletarian and non-proletarian ideas and an extremely complicated situation emerged. As Chairman Mao has said: **"In the past, we fought north and south; it was easy to fight such wars. For the enemy was obvious. The present Great Proletarian Cultural Revolution is much more difficult than that kind of war." "The problem is that those who commit ideological errors are mixed up with those whose contradiction with us is one between ourselves and the enemy, and for a time it is hard to sort them out."** Nevertheless, relying on the wise leadership of Chairman Mao, we finally overcame this difficulty. In the summer of 1967, Chairman Mao made an inspection tour north and south of the Yangtse River and issued most important instructions, guiding the broad revolutionary masses to distinguish gradually the contradictions between ourselves and the enemy from those among the people and to further promote the revolutionary great alliance and the revolutionary three-in-one combination and guiding people with petty-bourgeois ideas onto the path of the proletarian revolution. Consequently, it was only the enemy who was thrown into disorder while the broad masses were steeled in the course of the struggle.

The handful of renegades, enemy agents, unreformed landlords, rich peasants, counter-revolutionaries, bad elements and rightists, active counter-revolutionaries, bourgeois careerists and double-dealers who had hidden themselves among the masses would not reveal their colours until the climate suited them. In the summer of 1967 and the spring of 1968, they again fanned up a reactionary evil wind both from the Right and the extreme "Left" to reverse correct verdicts. They directed their spear head against the proletarian headquarters headed by Chairman Mao, against the People's Liberation Army and against the new-born revolutionary committees. In the meantime, they incited the masses to struggle against each other and organized counter-revolutionary conspiratorial cliques in a vain attempt to stage a counter-seizure of power from the proletariat. However, like their chieftain Liu Shao-chi, this handful of bad people was finally exposed. This was an important victory for the Great Proletarian Cultural Revolution.

III. ON CARRYING OUT THE TASKS OF STRUGGLE-CRITICISM TRANSFORMATION CONSCIENTIOUSLY

As in all other revolutions, the fundamental question in the current great revolution in the realm of the superstructure is the question of political power, the question of which class holds leadership. The establishment of revolutionary committees in all provinces, municipalities and autonomous regions throughout the country (with the exception of Taiwan Province) marks the great, decisive victory achieved by this revolution. However, the revolution is not yet over. The proletariat must continue to advance, **"carry out the tasks of struggle-criticism-transformation conscientiously"** and carry the socialist revolution in the realm of the superstructure through to the end.

101

Chairman Mao says:

Struggle-criticism-transformation in a factory, on the whole, goes through the following stages: Establishing a three-in-one revolutionary committee; carrying out mass criticism and repudiation; purifying the class ranks; consolidating the Party organization; and simplifying the administrative structure, changing irrational rules and regulations and sending office workers to the workshops.

We must act on Chairman Mao's instruction and fulfil these tasks in every single factory, every single school, every single commune and every single unit in a deep-going, meticulous, down-to-earth and appropriate way.

Confronted with a thousand and one tasks, a revolutionary committee must grasp the fundamental: It must put the living study and application of Mao Tsetung Thought above all work and place Mao Tsetung Thought in command of everything. For decades, Mao Tsetung Thought has been showing the orientation of the revolution to the whole Party and the people of the whole country. However, as Liu Shao-chi and his gang of counter-revolutionary revisionists blocked Chairman Mao's instructions, the broad revolutionary masses could hardly hear Chairman Mao's voice directly.

The storm of the present great revolution has destroyed the big and little "palaces of hell-rulers" and has made it possible for Mao Tsetung Thought to reach the broad revolutionary masses directly. This is a great victory. This wide dissemination of Mao Tsetung Thought in a big country with a population of 700 million is the most significant achievement of the Great Proletarian Cultural Revolution. In this revolution, hundreds of millions of people always carry with them *Quotations from Chairman Mao Tsetung*, which they study and apply conscientiously. As soon as a new instruction of Chairman Mao's is issued, they propagate it and go into action. This most valuable practice must be maintained and persevered in. We should carry on in a deep-going way the mass movement for the living study and application of Mao Tsetung Thought, continue to run well the Mao Tsetung Thought study classes of all types and, in the light of Chairman Mao 's *May 7 Directive of 1966,* truly turn the whole country into a great school of Mao Tsetung Thought.

All revolutionary comrades must be clearly aware that class struggle will by no means cease in the ideological and political spheres. The struggle between the proletariat and the bourgeoisie by no means dies out with our seizure of power. We must continue to hold high the banner of revolutionary mass criticism and use Mao Tsetung Thought to criticize the bourgeoisie, to criticize revisionism and all kinds of Right or extreme "Left" erroneous ideas which run counter to Chairman Mao's proletarian revolutionary line and to criticize bourgeois individualism and the theory of "many centres", that is, the theory of "no centre". We must continue to criticize thoroughly and discredit completely the stuff of the renegade, hidden traitor and scab Liu Shao-chi such as the slavish comprador philosophy and the doctrine of trailing behind at a snail's pace, and must firmly establish among the cadres and the masses of the people Chairman Mao's concept of **"maintaining independence and keeping the initiative in our own hands and relying on our own efforts",** so as to ensure that our cause will continue to advance in the direction indicated by Chairman Mao.

Chairman Mao points out:

The revolutionary committee should exercise unified leadership, eliminate duplication in the administrative structure, follow the policy of "better troops and simpler administration" and organize itself into a revolutionized leading group which maintains close ties with the masses.

This is a basic principle which enables the superstructure to serve its socialist economic base still better. A duplicate administrative structure divorced from the masses, scholasticism which suppresses and binds their revolutionary initiative, and a landlord and bourgeois style of going in for formality and ostentations--all these are destructive to the socialist economic base, advantageous to capitalism and harmful to socialism. In accordance with Chairman Mao's instructions, organs of state power at all levels and other organizations must keep close ties with the masses, first of all with the basic masses--the working class and the poor and lower-middle peasants. Cadres, old and new, must constantly sweep away the dust of bureaucracy and must not fall into the bad habit of "acting as bureaucrats and overlords". They must keep on practising frugality in carrying out revolution, run all socialist undertakings industriously and thriftily, oppose extravagance and waste and guard against bourgeois attacks with sugar-coated bullets. They must maintain the system of cadre participation in collective productive labour. They must be concerned with the well-being of the masses. They must themselves make investigation and study in accordance with Chairman Mao's teachings, "dissect" one or several "sparrows" and constantly sum up experience. They must make criticism and self-criticism regularly and, in line with the five requirements for the successors to the revolution as set forth by Chairman Mao, **"fight self, criticize revisionism"** and conscientiously remould their world outlook.

The People's Liberation Army is the mighty pillar of the dictatorship of the proletariat. Chairman Mao has pointed out many times: From the Marxist point of view the main component of the state is the army. The Chinese People's Liberation Army personally founded and led by Chairman Mao is the army of the workers and peasants, the army of the proletariat. It has performed great historic feats in the struggle for overthrowing the three big mountains of imperialism, feudalism and bureaucrat-capitalism, and in the struggles for defending the motherland, for resisting existing U.S. aggression and aiding Korea and for smashing aggression by imperialism, revisionism and the reactionaries. In the Great Proletarian Cultural Revolution, large numbers of commanders and fighters have taken part in the work of "three supports and two militaries" (i.e., support industry, support agriculture, support the broad masses of the Left, military control, political and military training) and representatives of the army have taken part in the three-in-one combination; they have tempered themselves in the class struggle, strengthened their ties with the masses, promoted the ideological revolutionization of the army, and made new contributions to the people. And this is also the best preparation against war. We must carry forward the glorious tradition of **"supporting the government and cherishing the people", "supporting the army and cherishing the people", strengthen the** unity between the army and the people, strengthen the building of the militia and of national defence and do a still better job in all our work. For the past three years, it is precisely because the people have supported the army and the army has protected the people that renegades, enemy agents, absolutely unrepentant persons in power taking the capitalist road and counter-revolutionaries have failed in their attempts to undermine this great people's army of ours.

Departments of culture, art, education, the press, health, etc., occupy an extremely important position in the realm of the superstructure. The line **"We must whole-heartedly rely on the working class"** was decided upon at the Second Plenary Session of the Seventh Central Committee. And now, at Chairman Mao's **call that "The working class must exercise leadership in everything",** the working class, which is the main force in the proletarian revolution, and its staunch ally the poor and lower-middle peasants have mounted the political stage of struggle-criticism-transformation in the superstructure. From July 27, 1968, mighty contingents of the working class marched to places long dominated by the persons in power taking the capitalist road and to all places where intellectuals were predominant in number. It was a great revolutionary action. Whether the proletariat is able to take firm root in the positions of culture and education and transform them with Mao

Tsetung Thought is the key question in carrying the Great Proletarian Cultural Revolution through to the end. Chairman Mao has attached profound importance to our work in this connection and personally grasped typical cases, thus setting us a brilliant example. We must overcome the wrong tendency of some comrades to slight the ideological, cultural and educational front; we must closely follow Chairman Mao and consistently do hard and careful work. **"On its part, the working class should always raise its political consciousness in the course of struggle"**, sum up experience in leading the struggle-criticism-transformation in the superstructure and win the battle on this front.

IV. ON THE POLICIES OF THE GREAT PROLETARIAN CULTURAL REVOLUTION

In order to continue the revolution in the realm of the superstructure, it is imperative to carry out conscientiously all Chairman Mao's proletarian policies.

Policies for the Great Proletarian Cultural Revolution were early stipulated explicitly in the Circular of May 16, 1966 and the 16-Point Decision of August 1966. The series of Chairman Mao's latest instructions including **"Serious attention must be paid to policy in the stage of struggle-criticism-transformation in the Great Proletarian Cultural Revolution"** have further specified the various policies.

The main question at present is to carry them out to the letter.

The Party's policies, including those towards the intellectuals, the cadres, **"the sons and daughters that can be educated"** [the sons and daughters of those who have committed crimes or mistakes--*translator*], the mass organizations, the struggle against the enemy and economic policy--all these policies come under the general heading of the correct handling of the two different types of contradictions, those between ourselves and the enemy and those among the people.

The majority or the vast majority of the intellectuals trained in the old type of schools and colleges are able or willing to integrate themselves with the workers, peasants and soldiers. They should be **"reeducated"** by the workers, peasants and soldiers under the guidance of Chairman Mao's correct line, and encouragement should be given to those who do well in such integration and to the Red Guards and educated young people who are active in going to the countryside or mountainous areas.

Chairman Mao has taught us many times: **"Help more people by educating them and narrow the target of attack"** and **"carry out Marx's teaching that only by emancipating all mankind can the proletariat achieve its own final emancipation"**. With regard to people who have made mistakes, stress must be laid on giving them education and reeducation, doing patient and careful ideological and political work and truly acting **"on the principle of 'learning from past mistakes to avoid future ones' and 'curing the sickness to save the patient', in order to achieve the twofold objective of clarity in ideology and unity among comrades"**. With regard to good people who committed the errors characteristic of the capitalist-roader in power but have now raised their political consciousness and gained the understanding of the masses, they should be promptly "liberated", assigned to suitable work and encouraged to go among the masses of the workers and peasants to remould their world outlook. As for those who have made a little progress and become awakened to some extent, we should continue to help them, proceeding from the viewpoint of unity. Chairman Mao has recently pointed out:

The proletariat is the greatest class in the history of mankind. It is the most powerful revolutionary class ideologically, politically and in strength. It can and must unite the overwhelming majority of people around itself so as to isolate the handful of enemies to the maximum and

attack them.

In the struggle against the enemy, we must carry out the policy **"make use of contradictions, win over the many, oppose the few and crush our enemies one by one"** which Chairman Mao has always advocated. **"Stress should be laid on the weight of evidence and on investigation and study, and it is strictly forbidden to obtain confessions by compulsion and to give them credence."**

We must implement Chairman Mao's policies of **"leniency towards those who confess their crimes and severe punishment of those who refuse to do so"** and of **"giving a way out"**. We rely mainly on the broad masses of the people in exercising dictatorship over the enemy. As for bad people or suspects ferreted out through investigation in the movement for purifying the class ranks, the policy of **"killing none and not arresting most"** should be applied to all except the active counter-revolutionaries against whom there is conclusive evidence of crimes such as murder, arson or poisoning, and who should be dealt with in accordance with the law.

As for the bourgeois reactionary academic authorities, we should either criticize them and see, or criticize them and give them work to do, or criticize them and provide them with a proper livelihood. In short, we should criticize their ideology and at the same time give them a way out. To handle this part of the contradictions between ourselves and the enemy in the manner of handling contradictions among the people is beneficial to the consolidation of the dictatorship of the proletariat and to the disintegration of the enemy ranks.

In carrying out the policies of the Party, all units must study their specific conditions. In places where the revolutionary great alliance has not yet been sufficiently consolidated, it is necessary to help the revolutionary masses bring about the revolutionary great alliance in accordance with revolutionary principles and on the basis of different fields of work, trades and school classes so that they will become united against the enemy. In units where the work of purifying the class ranks has not yet started or has only just started, it is imperative to grasp the work firmly and do it well in accordance with the Party's policies. In units where the purification of the class ranks is by and large completed, it is necessary to take firm hold of other tasks in keeping with Chairman Mao's instructions concerning the various stages of struggle-criticism-transformation. At the same time, it is necessary to pay close attention to new trends in the class struggle. What if the bad people get unruly again? Chairman Mao has a well-known saying: **"Thoroughgoing materialists are fearless."** If the class enemies stir up trouble again, just arouse the masses and strike them down again.

As the *16-Point Decision* indicates,

The Great Proletarian Cultural Revolution is a powerful motive force for the development of the social productive forces in our country.

Our country has seen good harvests in agricultural production for years running and there is also a thriving situation in industrial production and science and technology. The enthusiasm of the broad masses of the working people both in revolution and production has soared to unprecedented heights. Many factories, mines and other enterprises have time and again topped their production records, creating all-time highs in production. The technical revolution is making constant progress. The market is flourishing and prices are stable. By the end of 1968 we had redeemed all the national-bonds. Our country is now a socialist country with neither internal nor external debts.

"Grasp revolution, promote production"--this principle is absolutely correct. It correctly explains the relationship between revolution and production, between consciousness and matter, between the superstructure and the economic base and between the relations of production and the productive forces. Chairman Mao always teaches us: **"Political**

work is the life-blood of all economic work." Lenin denounced the opportunists who were opposed to approaching problems politically. **"Politics cannot but have precedence over economics. To argue differently means forgetting the A B C of Marxism."** (Lenin, *Collected Works, Chinese ed.,* Vol. 32, p. 72.) Lenin again stated: To put politics on a par with economics also means **"forgetting the A B C of Marxism"**. *(Ibid.)* Politics is the concentrated expression of economics. If we fail to make revolution in the superstructure, fail to arouse the broad masses of the workers and peasants, fail to criticize the revisionist line, fail to expose the handful of renegades, enemy agents, capitalist-roaders in power and counter-revolutionaries and fail to consolidate the leadership of the proletariat, how can we further consolidate the socialist economic base and further develop the socialist productive forces? This is not to replace production by revolution but to use revolution to command production, promote it and lead it forward. We must make investigation and study, and actively and properly solve the many problems of policy in struggle-criticism-transformation on the economic front in accordance with Chairman Mao's general line of **"Going all out, aiming high and achieving greater, faster, better and more economical results in building socialism"**, in accordance with his great strategic concept **"Be prepared against war, be prepared against natural disasters, and do everything for the people"** and with the series of principles such as **"take agriculture as the foundation and industry as the leading factor"**. We must bring the revolutionary initiative and creativeness of the people of all nationalities into full play, firmly grasp revolution and energetically promote production and fulfil and overfulfil our plans for developing the national economy. It is certain that the great victory in the Great Proletarian Cultural Revolution will continue to bring about new leaps forward on the economic front and in our cause of socialist construction as a whole.

V. ON THE FINAL VICTORY OF THE REVOLUTION IN OUR COUNTRY

The victory in the Great Proletarian Cultural Revolution in our country is indeed a very great one. But we must in no way think that we may sit back and relax. Chairman Mao pointed out in his talk in October 1968:

We have won great victory. But the defeated class will still struggle. These people are still around and this class still exists. Therefore, we cannot speak of final victory. Not even for decades. We must not lose our vigilance. According to the Leninist viewpoint, the final victory of a socialist country not only requires the efforts of the proletariat and the broad masses of the people at home, but also involves the victory of the world revolution and the abolition of the system of exploitation of man by man over the whole globe, upon which all mankind will be emancipated. Therefore, it is wrong to speak lightly of the final victory of the revolution in our country; it runs counter to Leninism and does not conform to facts.

There will still be reversals in the class struggle. We must never forget class struggle and never forget the dictatorship of the proletariat. In the course of carrying out our policies at present, there still exists the struggle between the two lines and there is interference from the "Left" or the Right. Much effort is still required to accomplish the tasks for all the stages of struggle-criticism-transformation. We must closely follow Chairman Mao and steadfastly rely on the broad revolutionary masses to surmount the difficulties and twists and turns on our way forward and seize still greater victories in the cause of socialism.

VI. ON THE CONSOLIDATION AND BUILDING OF THE PARTY

The victory in the Great Proletarian Cultural Revolution has provided us with valuable experience on how we should build the Party under the conditions of the dictatorship of the proletariat. As Chairman Mao has indicated to the whole Party,

The Party organization should be composed of the advanced elements of the proletariat; it should be a vigorous vanguard organization capable of leading the proletariat and the revolutionary masses in the fight against the class enemy.

Chairman Mao's instruction has determined our political orientation for consolidating and building the Party.

The Communist Party of China has been nurtured and built up by our great leader Chairman Mao. Since its birth in 1921, our Party has gone through long years of struggle for the seizure of state power and the consolidation of the dictatorship of the proletariat by armed force. Led by Chairman Mao, our Party has always stood in the forefront of revolutionary wars and struggles. Under the guidance of Chairman Mao's correct line, our Party has, in the face of extremely strong domestic and foreign enemies and in the most complex circumstances, led the proletariat and the broad masses of the people of China in adhering to the principle of **maintaining independence and keeping the initiative in our own hands and relying on our own efforts,** in upholding proletarian internationalism and in waging heroic struggles with one stepping into the breach as another fell, and it is only thus that our Party has grown from Communist groups with only a few dozen members at the outset into the great, glorious and correct Party leading the powerful People's Republic of China today. We deeply understand that without armed struggle of the people, there would not be the Communist Party of China today and there would not be the People's Republic of China today. We must forever bear in mind Chairman Mao's teaching: **"Comrades throughout the Party must never forget this experience for which we have paid in blood."**

The Communist Party of China owes all its achievements to the wise leadership of Chairman Mao and these achievements constitute victories for Mao Tsetung Thought. For half a century now, in leading the great struggle of the people of all the nationalities of China for accomplishing the new-democratic revolution, in leading China's great struggle for socialist revolution and socialist construction and in the great struggle of the contemporary international communist movement against imperialism, modern revisionism and the reactionaries of various countries, Chairman Mao has integrated the universal truth of Marxism-Leninism with the concrete practice of revolution, has inherited, defended and developed Marxism-Leninism in the political, military, economic, cultural, philosophical and other spheres, and has brought Marxism-Leninism to a higher and completely new stage. Mao Tsetung Thought is Marxism-Leninism of the era in which imperialism is heading for total collapse and socialism is advancing to world-wide victory. The entire history of our Party has borne out this truth: Departing from the leadership of Chairman Mao and Mao Tsetung Thought, our Party will suffer setbacks and defeats; following Chairman Mao closely and acting on Mao Tsetung Thought, our Party will advance and triumph. We must forever remember this lesson. Whoever opposes Chairman Mao, whoever opposes Mao Tsetung Thought, at any time or under any circumstances, will be condemned and punished by the whole Party and the whole country. Discussing the consolidation and building of the Party, Chairman Mao has said:

A human being has arteries and veins through which the heart makes the blood circulate, and he breathes with his lungs, exhaling carbon dioxide and inhaling fresh oxygen, that is, getting rid of the stale and taking in the fresh. A proletarian party must also get rid of the stale and take in the fresh, for only thus can it be full of vitality. Without eliminating waste matter and absorbing fresh blood the Party has no vigour.

With this vivid analogy, Chairman Mao has expounded the dialectics of inner-Party contradiction. **"The law of contradiction in things, that is, the law of the unity of opposites, is the basic law of materialist dialectics."**

Opposition and struggle between the two lines within the Party are the reflection inside the Party of contradictions between classes and between the new and the old in society. If there were no contradictions in the Party and no struggles to resolve them, and if the Party did not get rid of the stale and take in the fresh, the Party's life would come to an end. Chairman Mao's theory on inner-Party contradiction is and will be the fundamental guiding thinking for the consolidation and building of the Party.

The history of the Communist Party of China is one in which Chairman Mao's Marxist-Leninist line combats the Right and "Left" opportunist lines in the Party. Under the leadership of Chairman Mao, our Party defeated Chen Tu-hsiu's Right opportunist line, defeated the "Left" opportunist lines of Chu Chiu-pai and Li Li-san, defeated Wang Ming's first "Left" and then Right opportunist lines, defeated Chang Kuo-tao's line of splitting the Red Army, defeated the Right opportunist anti-Party bloc of Peng Teh-huai, Kao Kang, Jao Shu-shih and others and, after long years of struggle, has shattered Liu Shaochi's counter-revolutionary revisionist line. Our Party has consolidated itself, developed and grown in strength precisely in the struggle between the two lines, especially in the struggles to defeat the three renegade cliques of Chen Tu-hsiu, Wang Ming and Liu Shao-chi which did the gravest harm to the Party.

In the new historical period of the dictatorship of the proletariat, the proletariat enforces its dictatorship and exercises its leadership in every field of work through its vanguard the Communist Party. Departing from the dictatorship of the proletariat and from continuing the revolution under the dictatorship of the proletariat, it is impossible to solve correctly the question of Party building, the question of building what kind of Party and how to build it.

Liu Shao-chi's revisionist line on Party building betrayed the very essence of the Marxist-Leninist teaching on the dictatorship of the proletariat and of the Marxist-Leninist theory on Party building. At the crucial moment when China's

114

socialist revolution was deepening and the class struggle was extraordinarily acute, Liu Shao-chi had his sinister book *Self-Cultivation* republished and it was precisely his aim to overthrow the dictatorship of the proletariat in our country and restore the dictatorship of the bourgeoisie. When he copied the passage from Lenin on the necessity of the dictatorship of the proletariat, which we quoted earlier in this report, Liu Shao-chi once again deliberately omitted the most important conclusion that **"the dictatorship of the proletariat is essential"**, thereby clearly revealing his own counter-revolutionary features as a renegade to the dictatorship of the proletariat. Moreover, Liu Shao-chi went on spreading such reactionary fallacies as the theory of "the dying out of class struggle", the theory of "docile tools", the theory that "the masses are backward", the theory of "joining the Party in order to climb up", the theory of "inner-Party peace" and the theory of "merging private and public interests" (i.e., "losing a little to gain much"), in a vain attempt to corrupt and disintegrate our Party, so that the more the Party members "cultivated" themselves, the more revisionist they would become and so that the Marxist-Leninist Party would "evolve peacefully" into a revisionist party and the dictatorship of the proletariat into the dictatorship of the bourgeoisie. We should carry on revolutionary mass criticism and repudiation and thoroughly eliminate the pernicious influence of Liu Shao-chi's reactionary fallacies.

The Great Proletarian Cultural Revolution is the broadest and most deep-going movement for Party consolidation in the history of our Party. The Party organizations at various levels and the broad masses of Communists have experienced the acute struggle between the two lines, gone through the test in the large-scale class struggle and undergone examination by the revolutionary masses both inside and outside the Party. In this way, the Party members and cadres have faced the world and braved the storm and have raised their class consciousness and their consciousness of the struggle between the two lines. This great revolution teaches us:

Under the dictatorship of the proletariat, we must educate the masses of Party members on classes, on class struggle, on the struggle between the two lines and on continuing the revolution. We must fight revisionism both inside and outside the Party, clear the Party of renegades, enemy agents and other elements representing the interests of the exploiting classes, and admit into the Party the genuine advanced elements of the proletariat who have been tested in the great storm. We must strive to ensure that the leadership of Party organizations at all levels is truly in the hands of Marxists. We must see to it that the Party members really integrate theory with practice, maintain close ties with the masses and are bold in making criticism and self-criticism. We must see to it that the Party members will always keep to the style of being modest, prudent and free from arrogance and rashness and to the style of arduous struggle and plain living. Only thus will the Party be able to lead the proletariat and the revolutionary masses in carrying the socialist revolution through to the end.

Chairman Mao teaches us:

Historical experience merits attention. A line or a viewpoint must be explained constantly and repeatedly. It won't do to explain them only to a few people; they must be made known to the broad revolutionary masses.

The study and spread of the basic experience of the Great Proletarian Cultural Revolution, the study and spread of the history of the struggle between the two lines and the study and spread of Chairman Mao's theory of continuing the revolution under the dictatorship of the proletariat must be conducted not just once but should be repeated every year, every month, every day. Only thus will it be possible for the masses of Party members and the people to criticize and resist erroneous lines and tendencies the moment they emerge, and will it be possible to guarantee that our Party will always forge ahead victoriously along the correct course charted by Chairman Mao.

The revision of the Party Constitution is an important item on the agenda of the Ninth National Congress of the party. The Central Committee has submitted the draft Party Constitution to the congress for discussion. This draft was worked out jointly by the whole Party and the revolutionary masses throughout the country. Since November 1967 when Chairman Mao proposed that primary Party organizations take part in the revision of the Party Constitution, the Central Committee has received several thousand drafts. On this basis the Enlarged Twelfth Plenary Session of the Eighth Central Committee of the Party drew up the draft Party Constitution, upon which the whole Party, the whole army and the revolutionary masses throughout the country once again held enthusiastic and earnest discussions. It may be said that the draft of the new Party Constitution is the product of the integration of the great leader Chairman Mao's wise leadership with the broad masses; it reflects the will of the whole Party, the whole army and the revolutionary masses throughout the country and gives a vivid demonstration of the democratic centralism and the mass line to which the Party has always adhered. Especially important is the fact that the draft Party Constitution has clearly reaffirmed that Marxism-Leninism-Mao Tsetung Thought is the theoretical basis guiding the Party's thinking. This is a great victory for the Great Proletarian Cultural Revolution in smashing Liu Shao-chi's revisionist line on Party building, a great victory for Marxism-Leninism-Mao Tsetung Thought. The Central Committee is convinced that, after the discussion and adoption of the new Party Constitution by the congress, our Party will, in accordance with its provisions, surely be built into a still greater, still more glorious and still more correct Party.

VII. ON CHINA'S RELATIONS WITH FOREIGN COUNTRIES

Now we shall go on specifically to discuss China's relations with foreign countries.

The revolutionary struggles of the proletariat and the oppressed people and nations of the world always support each other. The Albanian Party of Labour and all other genuine fraternal Marxist-Leninist Parties and organizations, the broad masses of the proletariat and revolutionary people throughout the world as well as many friendly countries, organizations and personages have all warmly acclaimed and supported the Great Proletarian Cultural Revolution in our country. On behalf of the great leader Chairman Mao and the Ninth National Congress of the Party, I hereby express our heartfelt thanks to them. We firmly pledge that we the Communist Party of China and the Chinese people are determined to fulfil our proletarian internationalist duty and, together with them, carry through to the end the great struggle against imperialism, modern revisionism and the reactionaries of various countries.

The general trend of the world today is still as Chairman Mao described it: **"The enemy rots with every passing day, while for us things are getting better daily."** On the one hand, the revolutionary movement of the proletariat of the world and of the people of various countries is vigorously surging forward. The armed struggles of the people of southern Vietnam, Laos, Thailand, Burma, Malaya, Indonesia, India, Palestine and other countries and regions in Asia, Africa and Latin America are steadily growing in strength. The truth that **"political power grows out of the barrel of a gun"** is being grasped by ever broader masses of the oppressed people and nations. An unprecedentedly gigantic revolutionary mass movement has broken out in Japan, Western Europe and North America, the "heartlands" of capitalism. More and more people are awakening. The genuine fraternal Marxist-Leninist Parties and organizations are growing steadily in the course of integrating Marxism-Leninism with the concrete practice of revolution in their own countries. On the other hand, U.S. imperialism and Soviet revisionist social-imperialism are bogged down in political and economic crises and beset with difficulties both at home and abroad and find themselves in an impasse. They

118

collude and at the same time contend with each other in a vain attempt to redivide the world. They act in co-ordination and work hand in glove in opposing China, opposing communism and opposing the people, in suppressing the national liberation movement and in launching wars of aggression. They scheme against each other and get locked in strife for raw materials, markets, dependencies, important strategic points and spheres of influence. They are both stepping up arms expansion and war preparations, each trying to realize its own ambitions.

Lenin pointed out: Imperialism means war. **"...imperialist wars are absolutely inevitable under such an economic system,** *as long as* **private property in the means of production exists."** (Lenin, *Collected Works,* Chinese ed., Vol. 22, p. 182.) Lenin further pointed out: **"Imperialist war is the eve of socialist revolution."** (Lenin, *Collected Works*, Chinese ea., Vol. 25, p. 349.) These scientific theses of Lenin's are by no means out of date.

Chairman Mao has recently pointed out,

With regard to the question of world war, there are but two possibilities: One is that the war will give rise to revolution and the other is that revolution will prevent the war.

This is because there are four major contradictions in the world today: the contradiction between the oppressed nations on the one hand and imperialism and social-imperialism on the other; the contradiction between the proletariat and the bourgeoisie in the capitalist and revisionist countries; the contradiction between imperialist and social-imperialist countries and among the imperialist countries; and the contradiction between socialist countries on the one hand and imperialism and social-imperialism on the other. The existence and development of these contradictions are bound to give rise to revolution. According to the historical experience of World War I and World War II, it can be said with certainty that if the imperialists, revisionists and reactionaries should impose a third

119

world war on the people of the world, it would only greatly accelerate the development of these contradictions and help arouse the people of the world to rise in revolution and send the whole pack of imperialists, revisionists and reactionaries to their graves.

Chairman Mao teaches us: **"All reactionaries are paper tigers." "Strategically we should despise all our enemies, but tactically we should take them all seriously."** This great truth enunciated by Chairman Mao heightens the revolutionary militancy of the people of the whole world and guides us from victory to victory in the struggle against imperialism, revisionism and all reaction.

The paper tiger nature of U.S. imperialism has long since been laid bare by the people throughout the world. U.S. imperialism, the most ferocious enemy of the people of the whole world, is going downhill more and more. Since he took office, Nixon has been confronted with a hopeless mess and an insoluble economic crisis, with the strong resistance of the masses of the people at home and throughout the world and with the predicament in which the imperialist countries are disintegrating and the baton of U.S. imperialism is getting ever less effective. Unable to produce any solution to these problems, Nixon, like his predecessors, cannot but continue to play the counter-revolutionary dual tactics, ostensibly assuming a "peace-loving" appearance while in fact engaging in arms expansion and war preparations on a still larger scale. The military expenditures of the United States have been increasing year by year. To date the U.S. imperialists still forcibly occupy our territory Taiwan. They have dispatched aggressor troops to many countries and have also set up hundreds upon hundreds of military bases and military installations in different parts of the world. They have made so many airplanes and guns, so many nuclear bombs and guided missiles. What is all this for? To frighten, suppress and slaughter the people and dominate the world. By doing so they make themselves the enemy of the people everywhere and find themselves besieged and battered by the broad masses of the proletariat and the people all over the world, and this will definitely lead to revolutions throughout the world on a still larger scale.

The Soviet revisionist renegade clique is a paper tiger, too. It has revealed its social-imperialist features ever more clearly. When Khrushchev revisionism was just beginning to emerge, our great leader Chairman Mao foresaw what serious harm modern revisionism would do to the cause of world revolution. Chairman Mao led the whole Party in waging resolute struggles in the ideological, theoretical and political spheres, together with the Albanian Party of Labour headed by the great Marxist-Leninist Comrade Enver Hoxha and with the genuine Marxist-Leninists of the world, against modern revisionism with Soviet revisionism as its centre. This has enabled the people all over the world to learn gradually in struggle how to distinguish genuine from sham Marxism-Leninism and genuine from sham socialism and brought about the bankruptcy of Khrushchev revisionism. At the same time, Chairman Mao led our Party in resolutely criticizing Liu Shao-chi's revisionist line of capitulation to imperialism, revisionism and reaction and of suppression of revolutionary movements in various countries and in destroying Liu Shao-chi's counter-revolutionary revisionist clique. All this has been done in the fulfilment of our Party's proletarian internationalist duty.

Since Brezhnev came to power, with its baton becoming less and less effective and its difficulties at home and abroad growing more and more serious, the Soviet revisionist renegade clique has been practicing social-imperialism and social-fascism more frantically than ever. Internally, it has intensified its suppression of the Soviet people and speeded up the all-round restoration of capitalism. Externally, it has stepped up its collusion with U.S. imperialism and its suppression of the revolutionary struggles of the people of various countries, intensified its control over and its exploitation of various East European countries and the People s Republic of Mongolia, intensified its contention with U.S. imperialism over the Middle

East and other regions and intensified its threat of aggression against China. Its dispatch of hundreds of thousands of troops to occupy Czechoslovakia and its armed provocations against China on our territory Chenpao Island are two foul performances staged recently by Soviet revisionism. In order to justify its aggression and plunder, the Soviet revisionist renegade clique trumpets the so-called theory of "limited sovereignty", the theory of "international dictatorship" and the theory of "socialist community". What does all this stuff mean? It means that your sovereignty is "limited", while his is unlimited. You won't obey him? He will exercise "international dictatorship" over you--dictatorship over the people of other countries, in order to form the "socialist community" ruled by the new tsars, that is, colonies of social-imperialism, just like the "New Order of Europe" of Hitler, the "Greater East Asia Co-prosperity Sphere" of Japanese militarism and the "Free World Community" of the United States. Lenin denounced the renegades of the Second International **"Socialism in words, imperialism in deeds, *the growth of opportunism into imperialism"*.** (Lenin, *Collected Works*, Chinese ed., Vol. 29, p. 458.) This applies perfectly to the Soviet revisionist renegade clique of today which is composed of a handful of capitalist-roaders in power. We firmly believe that the proletariat and the broad masses of the people in the Soviet Union with their glorious revolutionary tradition will surely rise and overthrow this clique consisting of a handful of renegades. As Chairman Mao points out:

The Soviet Union was the first socialist state and the Communist Party of the Soviet Union was created by Lenin. Although the leadership of the Soviet Party and state has now been usurped by revisionists, I would advise comrades to remain firm in the conviction that the masses of the Soviet people and of Party members and cadres are good, that they desire revolution and that revisionist rule will not last long.

Now that the Soviet Government has created the

incident of armed encroachment on the Chinese territory Chenpao Island, the Sino-Soviet boundary question has caught the attention of the whole world. Like the boundary questions between China and other neighbouring countries, the Sino-Soviet boundary question is also one left over by history. As regards these questions, our Party and Government have consistently stood for negotiations through diplomatic channels to reach a fair and reasonable settlement. Pending a settlement, the status quo of the boundary should be maintained and conflicts avoided. Proceeding from this stand, China has satisfactorily and successively settled boundary questions with neighbouring countries such as Burma, Nepal, Pakistan, the People's Republic of Mongolia and Afghanistan. Only the boundary questions between the Soviet Union and China and between India and China remain unsettled to this day.

The Chinese Government held repeated negotiations with the Indian Government on the Sino-Indian boundary question. As the reactionary Indian Government had taken over the British imperialist policy of aggression, it insisted that we recognize the illegal "McMahon line" which even the reactionary governments of different periods in old China had not recognized, and moreover, it went a step further and vainly attempted to occupy the Aksai Chin area, which has always been under Chinese jurisdiction, thereby disrupting the Sino-Indian boundary negotiations. This is known to all.

The Sino-Soviet boundary question is the product of tsarist Russian imperialist aggression against China. In the latter half of the 19th century when power was in the hands neither of the Chinese people nor of the Russian people, the tsarist government perpetrated imperialist acts of aggression to carve up China, imposed a series of unequal treaties on her, annexed vast expanses of her territory and, moreover, crossed in many places the boundary line stipulated by the unequal treaties and occupied still more Chinese territory. This gangster behaviour was indignantly condemned by Marx, Engels and Lenin. On September 27, 1920, the Government of Soviets led by the great

123

Lenin solemnly proclaimed: It "declares null and void all the treaties concluded with China by the former Governments of Russia, renounces all seizure of Chinese territory and all Russian concessions in China and restores to China, without any compensation and forever, all that had been predatorily seized from her by the Tsar's Government and the Russian bourgeoisie". (See *Declaration of the Government of the Russian Socialist Federated Soviet Republic to the Chinese Government.*) Owing to the historical conditions of the time, this proletarian policy of Lenin's was not realized.

As early as August 22 and September 21, 1960, the Chinese Government, proceeding from its consistent stand on boundary questions, twice took the initiative in proposing to the Soviet Government that negotiations be held to settle the Sino-Soviet boundary question. In 1964, negotiations between the two sides started in Peking. The treaties relating to the present Sino-Soviet boundary are unequal treaties imposed on the Chinese people by the tsars, but proceeding from the desire to safeguard the revolutionary friendship between the Chinese and Soviet people, we still maintained that these treaties be taken as the basis for the settlement of the boundary question. However, betraying Lenin's proletarian policy and clinging to its new-tsarist social-imperialist stand, the Soviet revisionist renegade clique refused to recognize these treaties as unequal and, moreover, it insisted that China recognize as belonging to the Soviet Union all the Chinese territory which they had occupied or attempted to occupy in violation of the treaties. This big-power chauvinist and social-imperialist stand of the Soviet Government led to the disruption of the negotiations.

Since Brezhnev came to power, the Soviet revisionist renegade clique has frenziedly stepped up its disruption of the status quo of the boundary and repeatedly provoked border incidents, shooting and killing our unarmed fishermen and peasants and encroaching upon China's sovereignty. Recently it has gone further and made successive armed intrusions into our territory Chenpao Island. Driven beyond the limits of forbearance, our frontier guards have fought back in self-defence, dealing the aggressors well-deserved blows and triumphantly safeguarding our sacred territory. In an effort to extricate the Soviet revisionist renegade clique from its predicament, Kosygin asked on March 21 to communicate with our leaders by telephone. Immediately on March 22, our Government replied with a memorandum, in which it was made clear that "In view of the present relations between China and the Soviet Union, it is unsuitable to communicate by telephone. If the Soviet Government has anything to say, it is asked to put it forward officially to the Chinese Government through diplomatic channels." On March 29, the Soviet Government issued a statement still clinging to its obstinate aggressor stand, while expressing willingness to resume "consultations." Our Government is considering its reply to this.

The foreign policy of our Party and Government is consistent. It is: to develop relations of friendship, mutual assistance and co-operation with socialist countries on the principle of proletarian internationalism; to support and assist the revolutionary struggles of all the oppressed people and nations and to strive for peaceful coexistence with countries having different social systems on the basis of the Five Principles of mutual respect for territorial integrity and sovereignty, mutual non-aggression, non-interference in each other's internal affairs, equality and mutual benefit, and peaceful coexistence, and to oppose the imperialist policies of aggression and war. Our proletarian foreign policy is not based on temporary expediency; it is a policy in which we have long persisted. This is what we did in the past and we will persist in doing the same in the future.

We have always held that the internal affairs of each country should be settled by its own people. The relations between all countries and between all parties, big or small, must be built on the principles of equality and non-interference in each other's internal affairs. To safeguard these Marxist-Leninist principles, the Communist Party of China has waged a long struggle against the sinister big-power chauvinism of the Soviet revisionist renegade clique. This is a fact known to all. The Soviet revisionist renegade clique glibly talk of "fraternal parties" and "fraternal countries", but in fact they regard themselves as the patriarchal party and as the new tsars who are free to invade and occupy the territory of other countries. They conduct sabotage and subversion against the Chinese Communist Party, the Albanian Party of Labour and other genuine Marxist-Leninist Parties. Moreover, when any party, or any country in their so-called "socialist community", holds a slightly different view, they act ferociously and stop at nothing in suppression, sabotage and subversion and even in sending troops to invade and occupy their so-called "fraternal countries" and kidnapping members of their so-called "fraternal parties". These fascist piratical acts have sealed their doom.

U.S. imperialism and Soviet revisionism are always trying to "isolate" China; this is China's honour. Their rabid opposition to China cannot do us the slightest harm. On the contrary, it serves to further arouse our people's determination to maintain independence and keep initiative in our own hands, rely on our own efforts and work hard to make our country prosperous and powerful; it serves to prove to the whole world that China has drawn a clear line between herself on the one hand and U.S. imperialism and Soviet revisionism on the other. Today, it is not imperialism, revisionism and reaction but the proletariat and the revolutionary people of all countries that determine the destiny of the world. The genuine Marxist-Leninist Parties and organizations of various countries, which are composed of the advanced elements of the proletariat, are a new rising force with infinitely broad prospects. The Communist Party of China is determined to unite and fight together with them. We firmly support the Albanian people in their struggle against imperialism and revisionism; we firmly support the Vietnamese people in carrying their war of resistance against U.S. aggression and for national salvation through to the end; we firmly support the revolutionary struggles of the people of Laos, Thailand, Burma, Malaya, Indonesia, India, Palestine and other countries and regions in Asia, Africa and Latin America; we firmly support the proletariat, the students and youth and the masses of the Black people of the United States in their just struggle against the U.S. ruling clique; we firmly support the proletariat and the labouring people of the Soviet Union in their just struggle to overthrow the Soviet revisionist renegade clique; we firmly support the people of Czechoslovakia and other countries in their just struggle against Soviet revisionist social-imperialism; we firmly support the revolutionary struggles of the people of Japan and the West European and Oceanian countries; we firmly support the revolutionary struggles of the people of all countries; and we firmly support all the just struggles of resistance against aggression and oppression by U.S. imperialism and Soviet revisionism. All countries and people subjected to aggression, control, intervention or bullying by U.S. imperialism and Soviet revisionism, let us unite and form the broadest possible united front and overthrow our common enemies!

On no account must we relax our revolutionary vigilance because of victory or ignore the danger of U.S. imperialism and Soviet revisionism launching a large-scale war of aggression. We must make full preparations. preparations against their launching a big war and against their launching a war at an early date, preparations against their launching a conventional war and against their launching a large-scale nuclear war. **In short, we must be prepared.** Chairman Mao said long ago: **We will not attack unless we are attacked; if we are attacked, we will certainly counter-attack.** If they insist on fighting, we will keep them company and fight to the finish. The Chinese revolution won out on the battlefield. Armed with Mao Tsetung Thought and tempered in the Great Proletarian Cultural Revolution, the Chinese people in their hundreds of millions and the Chinese People's Liberation Army, with full confidence in victory, are determined to liberate their sacred territory

Taiwan and **resolutely, thoroughly, wholly and completely wipe out** all aggressors who dare to come!

Our great leader Chairman Mao points out:

Working hand in glove, Soviet revisionism and U.S. imperialism have done so many foul and evil things that the revolutionary people the world over will not let them go unpunished. The people of all countries are rising. A new historical period of struggle against U.S. imperialism and Soviet revisionism has begun.

Whether the war gives rise to revolution or revolution prevents the war, U.S. imperialism and Soviet revisionism will not last long! Workers of all countries, unite! Proletarians and oppressed people and nations of the world, unite! Bury U.S. imperialism, Soviet revisionism and their lackeys!

VIII. LET THE WHOLE PARTY, LET THE PEOPLE OF THE WHOLE COUNTRY UNITE TO WIN STILL GREATER VICTORIES

The Ninth National Congress of the Party is convened at an important moment in the historical development of our Party, at an important moment in the consolidation and development of the dictatorship of the proletariat in our country and at an important moment in the development of the international communist movement and world revolution. Among the delegates to the congress are proletarian revolutionaries of the older generation and also a great deal of fresh blood. In previous congresses of our Party there have never been such great numbers of delegates from the Party membership among the industrial workers, poor and lower-middle peasants, and of women delegates. Among the delegates from the Party membership in the People's Liberation Army are veteran Red Army fighters as well as new fighters. The delegates of Party members from among the Red Guards are attending a national congress of the Party for the first time. The fact that so many delegates have come to Peking from all corners of the country and gathered around the great leader Chairman Mao to discuss and decide on the affairs of the Party and state signifies that our congress is a congress full of vitality, a congress of unity and a congress of victory.

Chairman Mao teaches us:

The unification of our country, the unity of our people and the unity of our various nationalities,,these are the basic guarantees of the sure triumph of our cause.

Through the Great Proletarian Cultural Revolution our motherland has become unprecedentedly unified and our people have achieved a great revolutionary unity on the broadest scale under the great red banner of Mao Tsetung Thought. This great unity is under the leadership of the proletariat and is based on the worker-peasant alliance; it embraces all the fraternal nationalities, the patriotic democrats who for a long time have done useful work for the cause of the revolution and construction in our motherland, the vast numbers of patriotic overseas Chinese and our patriotic fellow-countrymen in Hongkong and Macao, our patriotic fellow-countrymen in Taiwan who are oppressed and exploited by the U.S.-Chiang reactionaries, and all those who support socialism and love our socialist motherland. We are convinced that after the present national congress of our Party, the people of all nationalities in our country will certainly unite still more closely under the leadership of the great leader Chairman Mao and win still greater victories in the struggle against our common enemy and in the cause of building our powerful socialist motherland.

Chairman Mao said in 1962:

The next 50 to 100 years or so, beginning from now, will be a great era of radical change in the social system throughout the world, an earth-shaking era without equal in any previous historical period. Living in such an era, we must be prepared to engage in great struggles which will have many features different in form from those of the past.

129

This magnificent prospect far-sightedly envisioned by Chairman Mao illuminates our future path of advance and inspires all genuine Marxist-Leninists to fight valiantly for the realization of the grand ideal of communism.

Let the whole Party unite, let the people of the whole country unite, hold high the great red banner of Mao Tsetung Thought, **be resolute, fear no sacrifice and surmount every difficulty to win victory!**

Long live the great victory of the Great Proletarian Cultural Revolution!

Long live the dictatorship of the proletariat!

Long live the Ninth National Congress of the Party!

Long live the great, glorious and correct Communist Party of China!

Long live great Marxism-Leninism-Mao Tsetung Thought!

Long live our great leader Chairman Mao! A long, long life to Chairman Mao!